Synchronicity as
Spiritual Guidance

Synchronicity as Spiritual Guidance

by
Mark Thurston, Ph.D.

ARE
PRESS

ASSOCIATION FOR
RESEARCH AND
ENLIGHTENMENT

A.R.E. Press • Virginia Beach • Virginia

A.R.E. Press
Sixty-Eighth & Atlantic Avenue
P.O. Box 656
Virginia Beach, VA 23451-0656

Library of Congress Cataloging-in-Publication Data
    Thurston, Mark A.
    Synchronicity as spiritual guidance / by Mark Thurston.
        p.   cm.
    ISBN 0-87604-377-5 (pbk.)
    1. Coincidence—Religious aspects. 2. Spiritual life. 3. I
Ching. 4. Cayce, Edgar, 1877-1945. I. Title.
BL625.93.T47   1997
131—dc21   97-631

Cover design by Lightbourne Images

Contents

PART ONE:
The Roots of Spiritual Guidance

PART TWO:
The I Ching with Wisdom from the Cayce Philosophy

Acknowledgments

The author wishes to thank Dianne and Dennis O'Keefe, compilers of *Change*, a booklet published in 1971 by the A.R.E. Press. Their work was the first to show how a linkage was possible between the Cayce material and the themes of the I Ching's sixty-four hexagrams. Their interpretation of the central message of each hexagram was the start of what was adapted and expanded for Part Two of this book.

The author also wishes to thank longtime friend and colleague Christopher Fazel, who collaborated on several aspects of the research needed to create this book.

INTRODUCTION

Decisions confront us every day. Some are almost trivial, but others have far-reaching consequences. Health care selections. Workplace options. Financial choices. Decisions about how to respond in relationships. Where can we get reliable guidance about these issues? Where do we turn for help in making important decisions?

This is a book about guidance resources, both the help that can come from the world around us *and* from our own inner life. It is designed to assist you to live in an often chaotic, confusing world that frequently demands tough choices.

For someone committed to personal spiritual growth, often those decisions are all the more complex and ambiguous. This book is especially for someone who wants to be responsibly involved with the physical world *but also* responsive to the invisible spiritual realm. In other words, the central purpose of this book is to put you in touch with reliable direction that furthers your purposes as a spiritual being.

The principle of synchronicity is to be our unifying theme. It is the concept of "meaningful coincidence," as Carl Jung defined it many decades ago. In a way that defies cause-and-effect logic, a series of outer events will sometimes match or coincide with each other *and* with an inner pattern of the soul.

What makes something synchronistic—and furthermore, a candidate for noteworthy guidance—it not so much the remarkable match of outer events but rather that profound intuitive sense that something *meaningful and revelatory* is at work.

Synchronicity is an encounter with an ordering principle of the universe. From the perspective of modern, mainstream thinking, the existence of synchronicity is nearly incomprehensible. And yet subjective human experience and some cutting-edge scientific thinking both point to the undeniable reality of a universal law which stands as a *complement* to the familiar rule of cause and effect. That additional principle is frequently at work to help us "put together the pieces of our lives."

In the chapters of this book you will explore a variety of ways in which synchronicity can operate to provide dependable direction for the choices you face. That synchronistic spiritual guidance can come in many ways: daily life events, dreams, prayer or meditation, psychic experiences, or more formal searches for direction such as with astrology or the I Ching, an ancient Chinese oracle.

The Format of This Book

Part One consists of seven chapters, each designed to take you a step further in understanding and making use of synchronistic guidance.The purpose of this first section is to provide an understanding of how you can work attentively and cooperatively with the principle of synchronicity. Included are models, examples, and suggestions for application. Background resources for these chapters are the groundbreaking ideas of Carl Jung, along with the best of transpersonal psychology, parapsychology, and spiritual philosophy.

The heart of Part One is the third chapter, which presents an eight-step formula for making a decision with the assistance of spiritual guidance. All of the methods and approaches described in the other chapters fit into the framework of this safe and practical way to engage spiritual direction in the process of decision making.

Whereas Part One serves as a handbook and training guide, Part Two takes the form of a reference book. Here you will find the ancient Chinese book of wisdom and guidance, the I Ching (or, Book of Change). Chapter 6 in Part One will provide an orientation to the I Ching and how to use it.

There are dozens of versions or translations of the I Ching. Why yet another? One feature makes this adaptation special: its integration of time-tested wisdom from the East alongside a source of twentieth-century Western spirituality. For each of the sixty-four hexagrams, you will find included a series of excerpts from the spiritual philosophy of Edgar Cayce, passages that reflect the key themes of that particular hexagram.

Edgar Cayce is one of the most significant figures of the twentieth century. His work provided a pivotal influence to the development of many important facets of human understanding today, including holistic health, parapsychology, transpersonal psychology, and an ecumenical approach to spirituality that retains the core of Judeo-Christian faith while integrating insights and practices from Eastern faith traditions.

Cayce was born in rural Kentucky in 1877, and for the first four-and-a-half decades of the twentieth century created a remarkable collection of teachings about natural healing, cosmology, and methods for soul growth. The *Journal of the American Medical Association* has referred to Cayce as the father of holistic health, and many theologians have recognized Cayce's pioneering work in forging a synthesis of Eastern and Western spirituality.

A self-educated and humble individual, Cayce had a method of presenting his ideas that was rather unusual. From the age of twenty-one he demonstrated the ability to alter his consciousness and receive inspired insights in response to specific needs or questions that had been addressed to him. After a period of sincere prayer in which he would rededicate himself to God's service, Cayce would recline and move into a sleeplike unconscious state, yet still responsive to suggestions or questions from someone at his side. He would speak aloud to the questions at hand, with a stenographer present to record his dictation.

These discourses, which came to be known as "readings," usually lasted about half an hour and filled up an average of four pages when typed. Over a period of forty-three years, verbatim records were made of some 14,306 of these discourses—all of them now fully available for study and research to anyone.

Although Cayce's method for presenting his ideas and teachings seems unconventional, it is not without precedent. Perhaps the most famous person to have exhibited a similar method was Thomas Aquinas. Aquinas's secretary and biographer noted that on occasion

Aquinas would sdrift into a sleeplike state from which he would continue to expound upon ideas, each of the sessions recorded by secretaries.

The Cayce material, in spite of the unconventional way in which it came into being, is one of the finest resources available to spiritual seekers or those who want a body-mind-spirit approach to health and healing. His philosophy is fundamentally consistent with the Taoistic principles expressed in the I Ching, especially in regard to the dynamic, unfolding nature of the universe. (For example, note the passage from Cayce on the fundamental quality of change, which appears on the opening page of Part Two.)

Part Two consists of two pages for each of the sixty-four hexagram patterns of the I Ching. Each two-page section has the Chinese pictograph and the number for that particular hexagram. A basic message or teaching for that hexagram is presented. Sometimes the term "sage" is used, referring to the wise individual who knows how to apply spiritual wisdom to the practical challenges of life. As readers and students of this oracle, we are invited to be like a sage by using the advice and insight from the I Ching in our decision making.

The parallel wisdom from Cayce is presented in the form of several excerpts keyed to the themes or key words of that particular hexagram. Keep in mind that each excerpt is usually just one or two paragraphs lifted from the verbatim transcripts of his discourses. Each excerpt has an identifying number that can be used to find the entire discourse from which it was drawn.

Getting Started

As you will see from stories related in Part One, I have often used synchronistic guidance for important decisions in my own life. I know, from repeated personal experience, that synchronistic spiritual guidance is very real and effective.

And, although spiritual direction frequently maintains an air of mystery and paradox, its accessibility and helpfulness is undeniable. You have only to look sincerely. An abundance of evidence will demonstrate that life is governed by a connecting, ordering principle that is constantly at work to help you find your way in life. All you need to get started with the ideas in this book are some heartfelt questions about how to live your life and a willingness to be shown the way.

Part 1

The Roots of Spiritual Guidance

1 / Was It More Than Just Coincidence?

W E LIVE in an orderly universe. Our lives are governed by universal principles and laws, none of which is inconsistent with the physical laws known to traditional science. All of these universal principles are underlying, unifying patterns from which our experiences spring.

This book is a study of how certain laws and principles shape our experience of personal guidance as we try to deal with practical decision making. Each and every day we make choices, most with little forethought or any sense that guidance is required. But on certain occasions we face a decision which has such importance or such a high degree of ambiguity that we clearly feel the need for help. It is in situations like these that universal laws can help us find a source of wisdom and understanding.

The Law of Oneness is probably the most important universal principle. It asserts the primary connectedness of all things. It suggests that the seemingly independent aspects of our lives are really part of a greater whole. They are linked by shared patterns of energy and fields of consciousness that may not always be immediately evident to our normal waking awareness.

Consider this example of interconnectedness. It involves four aspects in the life of a woman named Beth, none of which seems at face value to be linked to any other: her son, her secretary, a person met randomly in line at the bank, and a discussion she viewed on a late-night television show. The story of her day unfolded this way:

One morning at the breakfast table Beth listened to her son talk about his interest in fishing. It didn't seem particularly noteworthy, although it was unusual for her son to bring up this topic because he had not previously shown such interest in it.

Several hours later Beth was at her office desk when her secretary came in and asked for a day off the following week so that she could go on a fishing trip with her family. After nodding her approval to the secretary's request, Beth paused only briefly to note the match with her son's breakfast conversation, then she quickly got back to work.

At the end of the work day, Beth stopped at the bank on the way home. Standing in line for a teller, she struck up a conversation with the man in line ahead of her, only to discover that his occupation was charting deep-sea fishing excursions. She was surprised but didn't know what to make of this third occurrence.

Finally, that night as she was getting ready for bed, she flipped on the television remembering that a favorite celebrity was scheduled for a late-night talk show. Within the first three minutes of her watching, the talk show host told a story about his recent fishing trip.

Another story illustrates the same kind of coincidental occurrences. As Chris tells it:

"The other employees in my office were throwing a birthday party for me. They had put up balloons and streamers and they bought gifts and a cake. About ten o'clock we stopped work and commenced the festivities. However, this celebration was interrupted shortly after it started by moving men from an office supply company. My new desk had arrived, the new desk and chair which had been ordered for me a month before. They were delivering it at that very moment. Suddenly the whole office was astir with the commotion of shifting furniture around and getting me relocated and installed. In the middle of this activity my phone rang and on the other end was my wife Sharon telling me that she had just gotten news of a special gift. We had that morning received an invitation to do a conference together in England later that year. I knew that these separate events had no causal relationship. The office supply company had no knowledge of the fact that they were delivering my long-awaited new desk on my birthday, let alone at the very moment of my office party. The invitation to do the conference in England certainly wasn't timed by the sender to coincide with the other two events. Yet these events all did coincide to bring me a very meaningful message, Happy Birthday."

We have probably all had an experience like these two in some form or another—perhaps with four coinciding events as in Beth's example; or three, as in the story of Chris. The experience leaves us with the feeling that some force or influence is at work in our lives. It may leave us feeling that there is a "message" being delivered to us from many directions (e.g., Beth might interpret these events to mean that she ought to take up fishing). Or we may conclude that the *content* of the coincidences is of minor import, but that the real meaning is the reminder of how life *is* connected in its many aspects.

The Swiss psychiatrist Carl Jung coined the word "synchronicity" for this phenomenon of meaningful coincidence. It's a principle of connectedness which does not rely on cause and effect. Jung, of course, had no doubts about the validity of cause and effect as a law which governs most of our daily experience. However, his observations led him to the conclusion that there was surely more to the story of life. A complementary law was also a part of life. In Beth's story, it would be far-fetched to assume that the events with her son, her secretary, the man at the bank, and the talk show host had any causal relationship to each other. And yet, she experienced the events as similar in nature and linked in time (i.e., all in the same day).

Of course, not every coincidence is an example of synchronicity and its non-causal principle of connectedness. Consider this account from Chris who was cited in one of the stories above. "One day, while driving to work, I had to step on my brakes suddenly as I came to an unusually long line at the red light. When I finally got my chance to make the left turn, I suddenly had to brake again to avoid hitting a man on a bicycle who was ignoring the traffic lights. Within minutes, I had another near-miss from a car whose driver wasn't looking.

"Suddenly I asked myself, 'Am I experiencing an example of synchronicity? Is the universe trying to tell me something?' But I realized that these events were not 'synchronistic' in the true sense of the word. Although they contained a clear message to be careful on the road today, I could also identify a common cause. The summer season had begun in Virginia Beach, and the streets were full of tourists. My drive into work had suddenly been transformed into a summer obstacle course." These events were meaningfully related, to be sure, but they were also *causally* related—that is, the product of the law of cause and effect.

Synchronicity and Guidance

The stories of Beth and Chris share the feature of being spontaneous and seemingly unrelated to any pending decision. If there was any guidance to those synchronistic events, it would require some backtracking and self-study to identify the question or problem being addressed. On the other hand, individuals have known for millennia that guidance is available when one seeks help with a pressing concern. The orderly nature of the universe can often provide guidance and direction in the form of signs and synchronistic events.

Various forms of oracles and omens are excellent examples, and they can be found in most historical periods worldwide. Astrology is another good example, since one of the best ways to understand the validity of astrology is by seeing it as an expression of synchronicity.

From the very dawn of recorded history we find evidence that many people have assumed the existence of meaningful coincidence. Archaeologists have found written records dating as far back as 1830 B.C. which document the belief in astrology. From that time they have found tablets which list over 7,000 celestial omens and observations recorded by the first dynasty of Babylon. In other words, these ancient Babylonians believe that events in the sky such as the movements of planets had a meaningful relationship with events here on earth. Since there is no evidence that the planets physically cause events to happen, astrology is best understood as a complex expression of the synchronistic principle.

This fundamental belief that the movement of the planets are related to the course of human events seems to be practically universal among early civilizations. It can be seen in the legacy of Egypt, Greece, Rome, and China. The ancient stone monuments on the Salisbury plain of West Britain and the giant zodiac sculpted into the hills around Glastonbury demonstrate that as far north as the British Isles people in the ancient past believed there was a connection between events in the sky and events on earth. This belief also existed in the Americas. It's reported that when the Spaniards landed on the coast of South America the natives immediately welcomed them as visiting gods. They told their visitors that their ancient calendar foretold their arrival and they had been expecting them. Even the New Testament story of the birth of Jesus includes a special star which synchronistically heralds the event.

Astrology is probably the best-known example of the belief in synchronicity throughout history. However, it's not the only one. Throughout the primitive tribes of Northern Europe, tribal leaders sought guidance through the reading of runes. The leaders would go to a particular oracle or shaman and pose their question. The oracle would then cast on the floor a handful of stones on which were written various runes or letters which had symbolic meaning. The specific runes which turned up and the order in which they fell combined to provide insight and advice which the oracle then interpreted to the leader. This practice demonstrates the belief that the random arrangement of the runes had a meaningful relationship to the question that was posed. Since there is no clear causal relationship between the question and the casting of the runes, this relationship, if it exists, is clearly synchronistic.

A later version of this practice is the reading of tarot cards. The cards as we know them today probably came to Europe from the Middle East by the Crusaders of the eleventh and twelfth centuries. The cards contain pictures which carry symbolic meaning. The seeker or questioner shuffles the deck of cards and then hands them to the reader who lays them out according to a specific pattern. As in the reading of runes, the cards convey meaning according to which cards are turned up and where in the arrangement they fall. The reader of the cards interprets all of this information for the seeker who thereby gets guidance on a particular question. The principle of synchronicity operates here in the same way as it did in the reading of runes. The random arrangement of the cards determined by the shuffling of the deck is presumed to have a meaningful relationship to the question at hand, even though there is no logical or causal reason for this to be true.

Personal Examples of Synchronistic Guidance

In my own decision making I have often found synchronicity to be an ally. Often it comes when I'm least expecting it; on other occasions it arrives with a piece of an answer I am earnestly seeking. Two stories stand out in my memory, and I frequently share them with participants at workshops on spiritual guidance.

The first story was a powerful lesson to me about the need to be more alert for the signs and synchronistic occurrences all around me. It concerns a Native American medicine man and shaman named Rolling Thunder. Born into the Cherokee tribe, Rolling Thunder later moved to Nevada, where he served as the senior medicine man for the Shoshone and an eloquent spokesperson for Indian rights.

Rolling Thunder had an interest in Edgar Cayce's healing practice, and he said that before learning any of the particulars of Cayce's life and work, he had had an intuitive sense of a great medicine man who had worked on the East Coast in this century. Because he felt that something about Cayce's healing ministry resonated to his own, he made several trips to Virginia to learn more about Cayce and to speak to audiences assembled by the Association for Research and Enlightenment.

I first heard Rolling Thunder speak on New Year's Eve, 1971. As a part of his evening program for about three hundred people, he performed a healing ritual ceremony and worked on three individuals. It was a profoundly moving event for all who attended.

Rolling Thunder returned to Virginia the following summer to speak at a gathering of sixty-five college students and young adults at the A.R.E.'s camp in southwestern Virginia. In this setting, Rolling Thunder was able to take us out in nature, and he gave us instructions on how to be alert for and to recognize the signs of guidance found there. I had, of course, read about indigenous people's sensitivity to the ways that Spirit reveals itself to us in nature. But it was inspiring to get such firsthand teaching from a wise, skillful man like Rolling Thunder. He didn't call it "synchronicity," but I knew that Jung's term was just another word for the same thing. The flight of a bird in a certain direction was a sign of weather changes to come. The growth of a plant in a certain way was a sign about our group and the purpose of our being together at that very spot on that day.

Two years later I had a chance to build on this understanding. The memories of the A.R.E. camp lesson were still with me, but I had always assumed that those kinds of synchronistic indicators required being out in a natural setting, such as the wooded hillside of the camp. Somehow it seemed to me that the Great Spirit wasn't too fond of shopping malls, six-lane highways, and suburbia—the surroundings of my everyday life. It hardly seemed worth looking for such guiding signs unless I could get out into a more natural setting. But I was in for a surprise.

Now I was on the staff of the A.R.E. in Virginia Beach

and Rolling Thunder was scheduled to return. He agreed not only to give some presentations at the A.R.E. headquarters but also to travel afterward to a couple of other cities and meet with A.R.E. members. To my surprise it worked out for me to accompany him!

By the time we left Virginia Beach for our two-city tour, we had gotten to know each other a little bit, and I was starting to feel more comfortable playing the role of host for the upcoming programs. Traveling together on the airplane ride to Florida gave us a chance to talk at length, and I found Rolling Thunder to be very humble and personable, with a wonderful sense of humor but a determined vision about his work in the world. It certainly had to do with his healing work—but it was more than just fixing broken bodies. He realized that it was time for a healing within our nation among the various races and ethnic groups, and there was also a need for that kind of change worldwide.

When we arrived at our destination, local helpers drove us to the hotel where we would be staying that night and conducting a workshop the next day. No sooner had we checked into our respective rooms than I got a call from Rolling Thunder. Knowing that the hotel restaurant menu wasn't likely to include foods that he knew he needed, he thought the supermarket across the street looked inviting. He wanted to walk over with me right away.

Five minutes later we were ambling down the aisle of the grocery store. I was pushing the cart and he was walking along beside me, watching the shelves for needed items. But during those ten or fifteen minutes we were shopping, a remarkable conversation (for me, at least) went on. Rolling Thunder started pointing out to me situations and conditions in the store that he interpreted as meaningful signs. It was just like at A.R.E.'s camp in the woods, but this time in the middle of mod-

ern city life. The position or arrangement of food items
was a message about their appropriateness for purchase;
the movement of people at certain locations in the
store—something that looked random to me—was seen
by Rolling Thunder with a synchronistic flavor. I learned
that day that signs and synchronistic occurrences can be
found *anywhere.*
   Another story stands out in my memory of ways that
synchronicity has been helpful to me. Whereas the story
about Rolling Thunder had more to do with grasping the
scope of how signs and synchronistic events could be
recognized, the second account has to do with an important question. I was clearly in need of some guidance,
and synchronicity played a big part in getting my answer.
   It came at a time in my life when I felt like my spiritual
growth had stagnated. I wasn't slipping downward but I
was at a plateau and didn't seem to be able to continue
in my progress. For many weeks I prayed about this and
asked for guidance.
   One morning I went into the kitchen. On our window-
sill we had a little "word for the day" calendar, and I tore
off yesterday's word to see what the new one would be. It
was "vulpine." I closed my eyes and tried to think if I already knew what that meant. It looked a little bit like "lu-
pine"—related to wolves, but I really had no idea about
the meaning of this new word. So I opened my eyes and
read the fine print on the calendar page. The definition
of "vulpine" is "foxlike—of or related to a fox." I enjoyed
the feeling of learning a new word, but I doubted that I
would have occasion to show off my new vocabulary
addition any time soon.
   Thinking no more about it, I had my breakfast and finished getting ready for my workday. As I came into my
office about an hour later, my secretary greeted me and
then said, "You have just one appointment this morn-

ing. It's at nine o'clock with a man who's here to tell you about all the things A.R.E. has been doing wrong for the last ten years.

"Okay," I responded, " I'll be ready for him."

Sure enough, a man with just such an agenda showed up at nine. Upon sitting down to talk with me, the first words out of his mouth were, "When Hugh Lynn Cayce, as president of the A.R.E., allowed this Library and Conference Center to be built by Mr. Fox and his associates, he set in motion the forces of the anti-Christ into the A.R.E." He was referring to the very building in which the two of us were sitting at the moment.

I tried to think back some ten years to the time when construction was underway. In fact, I could remember the construction management trailer on the site, and it had the names Fox and Sadler, co-owners of the company.

But even though I could confirm in my memory this man's statement about a Mr. Fox being involved, I had no idea what he was talking about. "Why does that have anything to do with the anti-Christ?" I asked.

"Because Fox is 666 if you work with the letters of the alphabet numerologically. F is the sixth letter of the alphabet, and 0 and X also become 6s in the system that almost all numerologists use. Mr. Fox brought the 666 into this organization, I tell you."

At this point, with a part of my mind I was thinking, "How quickly can I get this appointment over with?" But with another part of my mind I realized, "How curious! The word for the day was vulpine, meaning 'foxlike.' And here synchronistically is 'fox' coming up again."

Soon thereafter the appointment ended. I was unable to give the man any information or promise of remedial action that would reassure him, and he left rather frustrated with me. The appointment ended with my still marveling at the coincidence.

Nothing else about a fox happened that afternoon, but as I was driving home about 5:30 I thought about the coincidence and tried to determine if there was a deeper message. I decided to challenge the Creative Forces, and I said silently within myself, "If there's really something to this, it's got to happen a third time."

When I got home I walked in the front door, and even before I went back to say hello to family members, I looked at the day's new mail that was stacked on a little table in the entrance foyer. One envelope caught my eye. From the return address on the outside I could see that it was from an organization in Washington, D.C., that we often supported with our contributions. It was a Christian-based hunger relief group. I thought maybe it was a letter with some good news that would lift my spirits because they often sent updates on successful new programs.

As soon as I opened the letter, I realized it was merely an appeal for additional funds because a return envelope was enclosed. But I began to read the letter anyway. I was immediately startled by the way it began: "Dear Friend, Foxes have their holes and birds have their nests, but Jesus had no place to rest His head . . . " It was an appeal for money to support a new shelter for the homeless, and they had chosen to use imagery from the Bible that began with a fox.

At that point I surrendered to the series of coincidences. There must be something to this. Three times in one day a fox has figuratively crossed my path.

That evening I began to try to work with that image symbolically, like a dream image. What was it saying to me about my problem, about feeling stuck on a plateau with my spiritual growth? As I worked with that image I began to see it had a message for me.

A fox, to my own consciousness, represents something clever; and there's a side of my mind that's very clever. In being willing to take a good, hard look at myself and my behavior patterns, I saw that in many ways I had begun to out-trick myself. In my cleverness I was finding ways of avoiding the sides of myself that I needed to confront in order to grow further. I was going to continue to be stuck on that plateau until I could disarm this foxlike nature in myself. Synchronistic guidance had clearly come to help me with a specific question that I had prayerfully worked on.

2 / Archetypes, Soul Patterns, and the Roots of Synchronicity

WHAT IS REALLY going on behind the scenes when meaningful coincidence occurs? How can we best understand the link between inner and outer events? Clearly, evidence suggests that sometimes it is not cause and effect. Some other type of connecting principle is at work. But what is that mysterious law of the universe that makes signs, omens, and coincidences so meaningful?

In the modern Western world, Dr. Carl Jung stands out as the pioneer thinker about meaningful coincidence. It is this Swiss psychiatrist who coined the term "synchronicity." The concept was first introduced by Jung to a private group of his followers in 1928, and two years later he first spoke publicly about the synchronicity theory. But only after more than two decades of careful observation and personal experience did he write a lengthy essay on the subject in 1952. It served to summarize his views on a connecting principle of human experience that stands in contrast to the familiar law of cause and effect. Jung realized in publishing such a theory that he would be open to ridicule because in many ways his principle of synchronicity violates the cherished and longstanding scientific model of reality. His opening words in the essay refer to making good on a promise that he had made many years before but only now had the courage to act on. He "conquered his hesitation" largely because the evidence for synchronicity had grown to such proportions that he could no longer remain silent about it. In fact, silence about such matters had not been his alone. As he notes in his foreword to the essay, "I was amazed to see how many people have had experiences of this kind and how carefully the secret was guarded."

Yet, Jung knew that there was growing data to support his novel idea. In this essay, entitled "Synchronicity: An Acausal Connecting Principle," he includes an analysis of emerging elements of science that are best explained with a universal law which *complements* (rather than contradicts) the familiar law of cause and effect. The parapsychology experiments of J.B. Rhine at Duke University are cited and examined in great depth by Jung. In these extraordinary laboratory experiments with gifted psychics, Rhine had produced findings that are virtually irrefutable. They point to a means of knowledge that seemingly operates outside of physical causality. Rhine lacked a theoretical explanation for how these striking demonstrations of telepathy, clairvoyance, and precognition were possible. Jung's law of synchronicity provided one possible framework.

Of equal or greater significance was the realm of

quantum mechanics and theoretical physics. Even though commonplace experience tells us that Newton's picture of the universe is perfectly adequate, cutting-edge physics in the twentieth century has opened up a whole new world of understanding. As Einstein showed, our universe is more relativistic than everyday experience might suggest. What's more, the solidarity and reliability we like to ascribe to physical life is actually much more elusive. Matter is rooted in probabilities, as quantum mechanics has discovered. What's "real" is not so fixed, and there is a measure of uncertainty to any observation we try to make of the material world. In fact, Jung's trailblazing essay in 1952 was co-published with an essay by the Nobel laureate and theoretical physicist Professor Wolfgang Pauli, who supported Jung's efforts regarding synchronicity.

And so, just as twentieth-century physics has required us to rethink the nature of the outer world, Jung challenges us to re-examine the laws that govern our inner world (and its relationship to our physical surroundings). It could be argued persuasively that Jung's law of synchronicity is for the psychology of the soul an equivalent in modern physics for the theory of relativity and the laws of quantum mechanics.

Jung opens his exposition of synchronicity in this classic essay by citing examples. First, he proposes a hypothetical one—perhaps not unlike real-life experiences of synchronicity for some people. He wonders with us, what is going on when I discover that the number on the ticket I buy for the city tramway matches the ticket number I have for the theater that night? Or, even more remarkably, that same number sequence might appear in a telephone number that is mentioned during the day. Jung reasons that "a causal connection between these events seems to me improbable in the extreme."

He follows this hypothetical illustration with two actual series of events in his own life. On Friday, April 1, 1949, he had fish for lunch. A companion mentions the European custom of making an "April fish" of someone. Earlier in the day, as part of his studies he had encountered a striking Latin phrase that links human nature to that of a fish. And, then in the afternoon, he met with a former patient whom he hadn't seen in months. She brought with her impressive pictures of fish which she had painted since they last met. In the evening he was shown a piece of embroidery with fishlike sea monsters on it. The very next morning, he met with another former patient—one whom he hadn't seen in years—and she told him a striking dream in which a large fish played the central role.

The second illustration doesn't contain as many coincidental events, but in many ways seems even more amazing. At a crucial point in her therapy with Jung, a woman patient dreamed that she was given a golden scarab—the sacred beetle of ancient Egypt. In the very moments when she was telling this dream to Jung, there was a tapping noise at the window of his office. He turned to see an insect knocking against the window pane from outside. He opened the window and caught the insect in his hand as it flew in—only to discover that it was a rose-chafer beetle, "the nearest analogy to a golden scarab that one finds in our latitudes."

These and many other similar experiences eventually led Jung to his law of synchronicity—the meaningful juxtaposition in time and space of events which are not linked by any explainable cause and effect. But Jung's theory is much more than merely a description of how outer world events seem to occasionally coincide. *He adds the inner element.* What makes something a case of synchronicity is the simultaneous occurrence of a certain psychological state with one or more external events. In the case of the scarab, it wasn't just the simultaneity of a dream being told and a beetle tapping at the window. The critical element was the psychological state of the woman as she intently relived her dream as she told it to her doctor.

Synchronicity and Archetypal Psychology

It is the inner element that leads us to Jung's most important contribution to an understanding of synchronicity. A deep soul pattern—what Jung called an "archetype" from the collective unconscious of humanity—is always involved in true synchronicity. This is *not* to say that the soul pattern is "causing" the simultaneity of several outer events. Since synchronicity is "acausal" (without a cause), then we shouldn't slip into cause-and-effect thinking, even if the cause comes from the invisible realm.

It's important to look more closely at the nature of these fundamental patterns of the human mind and soul—what Jung called archetypes. In his comprehensive study of Jung's theory of synchronicity, Dr. Ira Progoff points out that archetypes aren't really symbols or abstract pictures with a universal meaning, even though that's the way they've usually been explained. Instead, he emphasizes that the archetypes are more basic and fundamental than any image could ever be. We might liken this to the well-known fact that our spoken or written words are usually not adequate to convey fully what we're feeling or experiencing. Something deeper and more fundamental always stands behind the words. In a similar fashion, an archetype isn't merely a universal symbol that can easily be interpreted by consulting a dream dictionary. It's a potent factor in the human mind and soul that brings about *processes of change at profound levels.*

Jung himself described archetypes as being able to

"manifest themselves through their ability to organize images and ideas." They operate deep within us—patterning forces for the mind and soul, much like instincts are for the physical body. But their patterning effect is always operating unconsciously; and it's only in retrospect that we see them. This indirect way of encountering an archetype can happen as a powerful experience in a mysterious dream. Or, it can come, as we'll see, as an archetype participates in a synchronistic occurrence. What's most important, then, about an archetype is its *dynamic* quality. Progoff makes this point emphatically in his book *Jung, Synchronicity, and Human Destiny*, a volume that Jung himself commented on and edited. Progoff writes: " . . . in the final analysis it is incorrect to speak of archetypes as nouns . . . It is a correct description, however, to use the term as an adjective, for then we are speaking of the general archetypal effect that is brought about . . . " (p. 156)

So, for example, the archetype of the Great Mother resides deep in the soul mind of every person. It's a fundamental pattern of nurturance and care-giving. It has images and symbolic pictures through which it appears in our dreams or ancient myths. But that archetype isn't so much a rigid "thing" within us so much as a dynamic influence that frequently organizes our feelings and experiences, operating unconsciously and beneath the surface of our conscious awareness. However, as we'll see, that archetypal influence can become a player in synchronistic events, even the I Ching hexagram that one throws.

As mentioned above, Jung hoped to find, through his principle of synchronicity, something as lawful about the human psyche as the law of cause and effect is for the physical world. His groundbreaking work with synchronicity was meant to be for psychology and spirituality something just as important as Einstein's theory of relativity for physics. And the archetypes were to be a key player in Jung's new theory. In Progoff's analysis of the parallels, the physical world is given order and pattern through *mathematics*, and in a similar fashion the inner world of the human psyche is affected by the *archetypes*.

It's important, though, to return to the crucial point about the role an archetype plays in a series of synchronistic events. *The archetype does not cause the synchronicity.* Rather, that deep soul pattern is a *participant* in the occurrence, and *it imparts meaning.* Jung stated it simply this way: "Meaningful coincidence seems to rest on an archetypal foundation."

But how *does* an archetype "participate"? It serves to coalesce or to configure inner and outer events in such a way that *meaning* dawns in our consciousness. We can try to create a picture for ourselves of how this could happen, although any such effort must be at least as much poetic and metaphorical as it is logical. Think of the archetype's role during synchronicity by imagining it to be like a mediator. A cosmic pattern crosses a moment in time and serves as a focal point around which several small events in an individual's life can arrange themselves. Something universal is now touching the specific. It does not cause situations or occurrences in the person's life. But the situations form around them—in such a way that the alert and sensitive person can recognize at least a piece of the wisdom linked to that archetype.

To extend the earlier example, if the Great Mother archetype plays a participant role in your throwing hexagram #2 (Responsive Receptivity), it hasn't caused you to throw the coins the way you did. However, that archetype may have served the role of being a focal point around which can coalesce certain of your recent life events (inner and outer) *and* the throwing of the coins in a certain way. And then, if you are alert and sensitive, you may become more conscious of the wisdom and meaning that is imparted by that dynamic patterning force of the soul Jung called the archetype of the Great Mother.

This example illustrates a point made by Jung and his followers such as Progoff. We can't make synchronicity happen. If we could, it wouldn't be "acausal"—that is, without a cause. But we can discipline ourselves to be more open and responsive. Progoff eloquently describes what, in fact, is within our power to do: "It does seem to me to be possible to develop in a person an increased sensitivity to synchronistic events, and especially a capacity to harmonize one's life with such occurrences." (p. 132)

What's more, we can pursue methods, such as the I Ching, which *invite* synchronicity—but always keeping in mind that it is not we ourselves nor the coins to be thrown that cause or manipulate such coincidences, even though we are agents and participants in the process. And then, if we recognize something meaningful in synchronistic events, it's also up to us to *do* something with the insight that comes. We're challenged by any set of synchronistic occurrences to put the wisdom—no matter how small—into practical application.

Synchronicity and Science

Before leaving Jung's theoretical statements about the roots of synchronicity, it's interesting to note one further element of his groundbreaking essay "Synchronicity: An Acausal Connecting Principle." Apparently, he felt compelled to make some type of scientific demonstration of his own, not merely to cite J.B. Rhine's parapsychology work.

Jung and several associates undertook a statistical

analysis of comparative data based on astrological horo-
scopes of 325 married couples. He felt certain that there
was no physicalistic, causal relationship between the
position of a planet at one's birth and one's adult personality and behavior. However, he recognized that since
ancient times astrology had been a source of meaning to
many cultures in many time periods.

Jung was surprised to find that a statistically higher-
than-average number of the couples shared a particular
astrological relationship. An unexpectedly high number
of wives had their natal lunar postions in the same sign
as their husbands' natal sun. To Jung, this observation
seemed to be a clear example of synchronicity in action.
Although the statistical methods later came under attack
from some doubters, this experiment still stands as one
of the first attempts to apply the tools of modern scientific analysis to an ancient wisdom tradition. At the very
least, the results were suggestive that something authentic—such as a non-causal connecting princple—was at
work.

What other scientific theory or research evidence is
there to support the principle of non-causal connectedness? Is there any way to test the hypothesis that relationships exist between events, beyond what can be
explained by merely cause and effect?

In fact, one of the most surprising pieces of supportive evidence for the law of synchronicity comes from the
pioneering field of subatomic physics. The research in
this area is leading many physicists to adopt a rather
"holographic" view of the universe. In other words, some
recent experiments seem to demonstrate a "oneness" or
"wholeness" to the universe that defies the accepted
rules of cause and effect.

Tests in both mathematical theories and in the laboratory have demonstrated how subatomic particles respond and relate to one another's movement, even

though this relationship is *not explainable* in traditional terms of cause and effect. David Bohm, a professor of physics at Birbeck College, University of London, commented on the implications of these experiments this way: "Thus, one is led to a new notion of Unbroken Wholeness which denies the classical idea of analyzability of the world into separately and independently existent parts . . . " In other words, the universe cannot be divided into separate local events. All events are tied together in an unbroken wholeness.

While the Cayce readings never use the specific word "synchronicity," they do refer to the law of oneness which seems to be the same principle that Bohm describes. For example, this speaks of the oneness of life: "And in this awareness there comes the comprehending, the understanding that all life *is* one, all conditions then are relative as one to another." (1402-1) In another instance, Cayce restated the law of relative oneness and draws human experience into the picture: "As each and every atom in the universe has its relative relation with every other atom, then man's development lies in the relativity of all forces . . . " (900-70)

In spite of tantalizing bits of evidence from physicists or supportive theoretical positions from Jung, Cayce, and the cultural history of oracles, indisputable "proof" for synchronicity remains elusive. Perhaps the more important question is simply how people can best be aware of synchronicity and its guidance quality. Systematic research efforts are needed in order to collect and analyze personal experiences. With that view in mind, my colleague Chris Fazel and I developed a research project designed to determine if synchronous experiences could be recognized and even encouraged. It investigated three questions:

1. How many people would be able to recognize synchronous experiences happening in their day if they

paid careful attention to the natural flow of events?

2. Can the number of synchronous experiences actually be increased by such practices as meditation, attunement reveries, or observation exercises?

3. Can synchronicity provide meaningful guidance in solving a problem or making a decision?

The project covered a three-week period. It is described in chapter 7 so that anyone can follow the same steps. Chapter 7 also includes a brief report on some of the results with fifty-three participants, which showed overall favorable conclusions about our capacity to follow certain exercises and develop a more conscious relationship with synchronicity.

In brief, the research project's first week started with an educational effort in which participants were informed about the law of synchronicity through reading assignments and an instructive cassette tape. Then they spent the first week just keeping an eye out for coincidences and recorded their observations, along with any meanings that the events might have implied.

For the second week, they added two new elements to the research. First, they formulated a question in order to test whether synchronous events would provide guidance toward an answer. In addition to this, they were given a variety of enhancement exercises and invited to test their effectiveness in encouraging synchronous experiences. There were four exercises: listening to an attunement reverie, taking a random walk, exploring a library, and browsing through magazines or newspapers. The participants were asked to use at least one of these exercises each day, recording which they used along with any notable coincidences.

The third week continued the quest for guidance with the added help of a booklet based on the I Ching. The participants looked for any connections between the week's experiences and the booklet passage to which they'd been led. After the three-week project, each participant was asked to complete a report form and send it back.

More experiments like this one are needed—not so much to prove whether or not synchronicity is a reality but to understand how people can work more consciously with its presence in their daily lives. It is hoped that, after reading the remaining chapters of Part One of this book, you will be enthused about trying this research project.

3 / THE STEPS TO SPIRITUAL GUIDANCE

THE TWENTIETH century has seen many individuals famed for their skill at providing guidance. Religious figures, psychologists and counselors, newspaper advice columnists, and clairvoyants. Probably none has done more to advance our understanding of guidance from a spiritual perspective than has Edgar Cayce, Christian mystic, holistic healing guide, and spiritual growth advisor to thousands.

The organization that he founded in 1931—the Association for Research and Enlightenment—has always been a place where people came looking for spiritual guidance. When Edgar Cayce was alive to give his guidance-laden discourses, people wrote and people came to Virginia Beach looking for direction from this man on a remarkable array of problems: health concerns, career crises, problems with relationships, financial disasters, questions about the meaning of life. And since Edgar Cayce's death in 1945, the A.R.E. has continued to focus on spiritual guidance, now by teaching people the tools by which they can begin to get their own answers from within.

The methodology is based on a wonderful promise found in the Cayce teachings about spiritual guidance. More important than any technique we can learn and practice is a promise about guidance: We can make contact directly with God.

Cayce was asked by one inquirer, "What is the highest possible psychic realization? His answer emphasized the capacity we have to make an immediate and personal connection with our Creator: That God will speak directly with each one of us. We can make contact with the very highest source, for any kind of problem we may have. Spiritual guidance is available to everyone.

What is meant by "spiritual guidance"? One way is to see it as a special quality of information that comes to help us. It's information that doesn't rest upon a materialistic understanding of life. Spiritual guidance never denies that we are part of the material world, but it comes from a source that is beyond just a material perspective of life. Another way of saying this is that spiritual guidance comes from the invisible side of life, from the unseen side of life.

But perhaps the most important definition that the Cayce readings gave of spiritual guidance is "information that comes to help us and which engages our own spirit." That's what makes it spiritual guidance. It's not so much a matter of where it comes from, but how it *engages* us. It touches us at the level of our ideals and our values and our motives. And that's why it's spiritual guidance.

Personal ideals will be a center point of all the methods of spiritual guidance to be explored in this book, including synchronicity. That is to say, we obtain, evaluate, and act on guidance best if we've identified a core value that we aspire to. The following question-and-answer exchange between a seeker and Cayce illustrates the point of just how important ideals are to the guidance process. In this instance, the purported source of guidance was rather unusual—an invisible "spirit guide"— but the principle Cayce emphasized was universally applicable. No matter what the apparent source of our guidance, the content of the guiding message had better resonate to our own core value, our own ideal.

(Q) Is Abdulla, the guide that I have, a worthy one to work with?
(A) Only when such influences are kept in accord with your own ideal are they worthy; but keep thine own ideal! For each soul must answer to self and the consciousness within! 1387-1

Cayce didn't deny that some spiritual being might be helping her from the invisible side of life. But he brought her attention back to the role her own ideals and motives play in any effective decision making. That advice is applicable to all of us who are interested in spiritual guidance, not just someone who believes he or she has a spirit guide. Whether we're working with meditation guidance or dream guidance or professional psychics or synchronistic signs or inspirational writing—any form of spiritual guidance always comes back to the necessary foundation of a personal spiritual ideal, a topic to be explored more deeply in chapter 5.

Personal Reflections on Spiritual Guidance

As I was in the process of developing workshop materials on spiritual guidance a number of years ago, I took a morning walk with my wife, Mary, and as we were walking I told her what I was doing that day. We began to talk about times in our marriage and our lives together when we felt that we had been guided spiritually. I asked her to try to identify with me what some of the characteristics of spiritual guidance had been.

Our short list may not be identical to the list of the characteristics someone else or some other couple might experience. But consider these features that she and I noted. Do they strike a chord of truth for you as well?

We saw that when spiritual guidance had come to us it always seemed to engage some way of understanding a problem that had not occurred to us yet at a conscious level. It's as if some source of knowledge was awakening, something that we experienced as wiser than our conscious rational intellects.

A second characteristic is related to the first. Spiritual guidance which has been accurate and reliable has always seemed to demand of us a little more than our conscious personality selves might have been willing to do. It was always a little bit of a soul stretch for us to follow that spiritual guidance.

A third and final characteristic we identified was the way in which signs or synchronistic events had often come up to reinforce or remind us of the appropriateness of the guidance we felt that we had received. Not only was it an inner prompting; there were usually outer signs also to confirm that we were on the right track.

I sometimes like to take the phrase "spiritual guidance" and adapt it a little bit, asking people to consider a slightly different phrase: *the spirit of guidance.* What would it mean to approach a problem in your life in the spirit of guidance? To me this has something to do with *openness and a willingness to be shown a better way.*

My own professional training is in psychology, and, in counseling people, I find that there are individuals who come with this spirit of guidance fully in place. There are others, however, who come seemingly looking for help but who don't come in that spirit, who aren't ready to hear a better answer—from me *or* from themselves. Think about your own life. If you have a difficulty or problem, you might turn to the I Ching, or dreams, or a professional intuitive, or meditation, or any of the other forms of spiritual guidance. Can you approach the process in the *spirit* of guidance, with an openness and a willingness to put aside your preconceptions and to be open to a new way of seeing that issue? That's sometimes easier said than done.

Oftentimes we are attached to the problem, and it's hard for us to imagine not having that problem in our lives anymore. The spirit of guidance requires of us a willingness to let go of the past and to let go of our difficulties and our problems. And it also means letting go of our prejudices and our biases and our preconceived notions of how that problem is going to be resolved.

The spirit of guidance is really rather paradoxical. It asks us to be humble on the one hand and yet also to have confidence—that there is a source of wisdom within and without. In the same bipolar fashion, it asks us to be receptive but also then to be willing to be active and apply the guidance that comes. So it's both humility with confidence and also receptivity with a readiness to act.

There are several other key ideas in the Cayce teachings about spiritual guidance—principles that provide a context or a background before we get into the methods of spiritual guidance. Cayce always emphasizes a need for balance between logic and intuition. As we come into the "house of spiritual guidance," figuratively speaking, we're *not* going to "check at the door" our logic and analytical abilities. We're going to need to be able to make use of our analysis skills along with our intuitive capacity to tune in to the invisible side of life. It's always this balance of working with both sides of the brain, so to speak.

Another key idea from Cayce's philosophy about guidance is just how *accessible* inner wisdom really is. In the so-called "work readings"—intuitive discourses that Edgar Cayce gave about the purposes and operation of his organization, the A.R.E.—he describes his own work in a unique way. It's a matter of teaching other people about the accessibility of this kind of information for all of us: " . . . the simplicity of the ability of individuals to apply that as may be obtained from their own subconscious self . . . " (254-46)

A final point to set a foundation about spiritual guidance is the freedom of will. Even when we've noticed a synchronistic sign, gotten an insightful dream, received an informative psychic reading, or tapped into meditative wisdom, *we still have free will.* We still have to use conscious judgment, and we have to recognize that we have a freedom of choice about how we'll go about applying that information. The importance of this faculty of the soul called free will cannot be emphasized too much.

On one occasion when he addressed the topic of how spiritual guidance works, Cayce even estimated the degree to which outward factors influence the course of our lives versus the influence coming from our own free will. In this case he was analyzing the effect measured by methods such as palmistry, astrology, and other types of esoteric indications of guidance. But I believe this principle relates to all forms of guidance that we can turn to.

(Q) What value is there in palmistry? To what extent may it be relied upon?

(A) As we have given in regard to any and every omen, it is an indication—yes. As to whether or not it will come to pass depends upon what the body, the mind of such an one does *about* that it knows in relationship to itself. It may be depended upon, then, about twenty percent as being absolute—and about eighty percent "chance" or what a body does with its opportunities. 416-2

Those last few words in the answer—"what a body does with its opportunities"—was his way of referring to free will. According to this teaching, the signs and indications that we can get from an astrology chart that offers guidance, or from an I Ching hexagram interpretation, or even a dream coming from within ourselves, still allow 80 percent of the influence to come from our free will. The 20 percent that can be measured or indicated by guidance tools is certainly significant, but these influences don't run our lives, unless we surrender our free will and drift with the flow of events.

A Practical Program for Spiritual Guidance

In the numerous case histories where Cayce offered spiritual counsel, he always emphasized the individual's capacity to get his or her own guidance in the future. He didn't want people to become dependent on him. And in many of those discourses, he presented a multiple-step process for making a decision under the influence of spiritual guidance. It's an eight-step formula that is straightforward and easy to follow.

1. The first step is to clarify your spiritual ideal. Here's where purposes and motives play a role. It has already been emphasized just how important that is. In chapter 5 you'll find details about how to set (or reset) for yourself a core value or a spiritual ideal.

2. Next is to formulate carefully your question. Write

it down. We may tend to gloss over this one and much too quickly assume we've clarified what we're looking for. It's important to articulate *precisely* what it is you want to know. Too easily one's question becomes something vague, such as, "What do I do with this problem relationship?" or "What can I do about my career?" Instead, it's important to articulate specifically what it is you want to know. "Should I start expressing the anger I've been feeling in my relationship with Tom?" Or, "Is now the time to start going to night school in childhood education so that I can be ready for a career switch in two years?" Carefully word your question. It can be formulated so that the answer must be a *yes* or *no;* and, in fact, Cayce often recommended that it be done that way. But many people get very good results by just working with open-ended questions, too.

3. Once you have your question written down, step three is to consider consciously all the facts that you have available. Collect the information that's available to you with your conscious senses and your rational mind. This is where you do your homework before looking for spiritual guidance.

4. Collecting all the facts might take ten minutes or ten weeks, depending on the question. Then you're ready to move on. Arrive at a *tentative or preliminary conscious decision:* a yes or no. Or, if it's more of an open-ended question, what you now think would be the best answer. Then measure that preliminary decision against your ideal: Could you stay in keeping with your spiritual ideal and act on what you have decided? If you couldn't, you need to go back and redo these first four steps.

5. Assuming you could potentially act on your preliminary decision and still be in harmony with your core value (your ideal), then you're ready to move on to step five, seeking guidance—both inner guidance and outer guidance. In this book we'll explore methods such as

synchronicity and other approaches by which spiritual direction can come. Step five is where you'd especially want to be alert for synchronistic signs or where you'd employ the guidance tools to be outlined later.

6. Once you've made use of two, three, or even more of these guidance modalities, then you're ready to assemble the information and insights that you've received. This comparative analysis will work best if you've been keeping a journal record of your results with the various approaches to guidance.

Evaluate each kind of guidance you've received. Rate its feeling of reliability. Look for patterns or repeated themes. What does the guidance seem to indicate?

7. Having made your evaluation of the different elements of guidance, now it's time to make a decision. That choice will perhaps reaffirm your tentative decision from step four. Maybe it will be only a slight refinement. Sometimes the guidance will have pointed in an entirely new direction. Here's where you make your guided decision.

Then, before moving on, subject your decision to a comparison with your spiritual ideal. Could you act on this decision and still be in harmony with your core value? If the answer is yes, proceed. But if something doesn't feel right and would require you to compromise your standards, then go back to step five.

Once again, as you evaluate the guidance and as you move toward a guided decision, you need always to measure what you've received against your spiritual ideal.

8. When you feel as though you've made a guided decision you could act upon, then it's necessary to go out and apply it. Too often people work with the first seven steps, and they are amazed at what specific guidance they can get. Then they never get on with acting on it! They're fascinated with how well the first seven steps work, but they fail to put the decision into motion with actions.

But even those who move on and try to apply the guided decision need to remember another point: It's very important to continue *to stay open* to further guidance. Stay on guard against any tendency to act like a bull in a china closet who stubbornly charges ahead— "Come hell or high water I've got my guidance, I'm going to make it happen."

Instead, we need to recognize that sometimes the guidance comes to us incrementally. At first it points us in the right direction. And as we begin to apply the first-stage guidance, more can come to us, refining the course of action. It's a continual recycling through these steps— particularly for some of the deeper problems and issues that we have in our lives.

Consider this analogy. Suppose you were in Denver, interested in driving your car to Virginia Beach, Virginia. If I were asked to be a source of guidance for your trip, I might talk to you on the phone as you got ready to leave, saying, "Get on Interstate 70 headed east and call me again when you reach the Mississippi River in St. Louis." The first experience of guidance hasn't given you the entire answer, but it has pointed you in the right direction and given you a step to apply.

After driving for a day or two, you call and ask for more help. This time I instruct you to get over onto Interstate 64 headed east and travel until you get to the Virginia state line. After another day or two of following my guidance, you reach the prescribed point where it's time for more instruction. Once again we talk on the phone, and this time I give you the directions to move across the state and eventually end up in Virginia Beach.

Admittedly, in this analogy one could wonder, why not give the driver all the directions right at the start? They could be carefully written down and followed all the way to the destination. But the experience of many people has shown that more often than not the guiding spirit within us doesn't work that way. Maybe our capacity to remember all the details is limited. Perhaps we might get discouraged or overwhelmed if all the aspects of a solution were presented at once. Or maybe it's simply because we're more likely to act on guidance when it comes to us incrementally.

An Example of the Eight-Step Guidance Process

Here's an illustration of working with these steps for guidance, a personal story. It concerns an important decision that I made as a young adult that resulted in my starting a career working directly with the Cayce material and the organization Edgar Cayce founded, the A.R.E.

Through my college years I was involved in Search for God study groups in the two cities where I went to college in Texas. These groups—usually with six to twelve members who meet weekly—were pioneered by Cayce and his supporters in the 1930s. Since then, they have been started in towns and cities all over the world. The purpose of such a group is positive character development and soul growth for each of its members.

As I was nearing graduation from college in the spring of 1972, I realized I faced a decision. I had a clear spiritual ideal for my life—"Christ's loving service"—but I began to recognize that I had an important decision to make. How was I going to start putting that ideal into practice? What was I going to do next, upon graduation? The members of my study group, all of whom were fellow college students, encouraged me to work with the guidance and decision-making sequence that is found in the Cayce material.

I literally wrote out my question: What am I going to do upon graduation? Then I spent a lot of time collecting facts about possibilities for what I could do. And as I collected facts, it seemed as if it really boiled down to three different options. One was to go on to graduate school. Another was to look for a job—that is, to start working right away. And a third option was to travel around the country and "find myself," as people of my generation called it back then. (I have since discovered, as I travel frequently with my job, that more often than not I "lose myself" in hotels and airplanes and don't know where I am some mornings when I wake up. But twenty-five years ago that option seemed very glamorous to consider!)

Having collected information and facts about all these options, I finally arrived at a preliminary conscious decision: I was going to look for a job and try to work for a while. The only place I knew of that I would be very enthused about working was at the A.R.E. in Virginia Beach. I had previously visited this center of the Cayce work and had attended some conferences. I'd met many of the leaders of the organization, and I thought I'd risk making a move and hope for a job.

With that as my preliminary decision, I went to the next Search for God study group meeting and told my fellow members about my provisional decision. They encouraged me now to start looking for inner and outer guidance. I prayed, I meditated, and I watched for signs. And before too long I had a very dramatic dream that seemed to speak directly to my question.

In my dream I was sitting at a table, and right across the table from me was Edgar Cayce's grandson, Charles Thomas Cayce, whom I had met at conferences and gotten to know a little bit. In the dream we were talking about his needs at A.R.E. and how he was on the verge of hiring someone to work with him.

I quickly replied, "Oh, hire me!" I was very enthusiastic and ready to promote myself as his assistant or work with him in some way.

We talked about this in the dream, and the last thing I can remember him saying was that he really had somebody else in mind, and he named another individual I knew. He wasn't going to hire me; he was going to hire this other person, and I could just forget it.

When I awakened from that dream, I was really discouraged but, at the same time, quite impressed with how specific dream guidance could be. I went back to my study group the next Wednesday night and told them this dream, and they all agreed, the process works. "It wasn't what you were hoping to hear," they told me, "but look at the guidance and how specific it was."

Based on that dream, I began to set in motion working on one of the other options, and I sincerely began to act on what I thought was authentic guidance. About eight or nine days later I had a second dream. In the second dream I was walking down a sidewalk and I saw up ahead, walking toward me, Charles Thomas Cayce again. Not knowing that I was dreaming, I hollered out to him, "Charles Thomas, hi! I had a dream about you the other night."

He called back to me, "Oh, hi—I remember that dream." And as he approached me, he came right up to me and continued, "But you forgot the second half of the dream."

"What do you mean?" I replied. "Tell me the rest of the dream."

He went on to explain, "Well, when I told you that you couldn't have the job, you didn't like my answer. And you went out and got a file that documented everything you've been doing for the last five years. I read it and was so impressed that I changed my mind. I said you could have the job!"

And so, in this second dream, I felt wanted and needed. I quickly announced to him, "That's great! When does the job start?" He replied, "Christmas day, this year."

"Well, what will the job be?" I wondered aloud.

He answered, "Your job title will be 'in charge of college-age young people who are looking for God.' " Strange as that may sound now, in the dream it sounded perfectly normal. I then woke up from the dream, obviously very excited. I couldn't wait for the next Wednesday to roll around so that I could tell my fellow study group members.

At the next meeting we talked about it. We measured the new guidance against my ideal. It seemed like the thing to do was act on it and to move to Virginia, which is exactly what I did in the fall of 1972. It was all I could do to keep from going up and making an appointment with Charles Thomas to tell him this dream saying, "You promised me. Now where is my job?"

But I did not do that, and at first there was no job. He did have some small, miscellaneous tasks that I could do—a project here for three weeks and something else for two weeks. But in early December of 1972 someone decided to leave his staff position to go back to graduate school. I applied for that job and got it. What's more, the job started New Year's Day, 1973, and the job title was Youth Activities Coordinator, which is very close to what the dream had predicted. Even more startling, it was within seven days of that Christmas date that the dream had given.

The point of this story is not to convince anyone that there's a divine purpose behind my having moved to Virginia to work where I am. Rather, the story simply illustrates a process about accurately deciphering guidance when it comes. Probably we all have a certain anxiety about misinterpreting guidance when we receive it. Over and over again I've observed a principle in my own life and in the lives of others. In essence that principle says that sincerity of application protects you from misinterpretation *if* you stay open for more guidance to come. In other words, your first responsibility is to try to apply the best understanding you have of the guidance. But in so doing, you must also keep alert for further direction. Even if you've misunderstood the initial guidance, you can get correcting, additional guidance if you're doing your best to interpret and act on what you've already received.

That principle is crucial to keep in mind as you start to work on Cayce's eight-step guidance procedure for one of your own problems or concerns. It's a safe, reliable approach if you have a clear, personal ideal and sincerely make efforts to apply what you learn. In the next chapter are details about the specific methods by which some of that guidance may come.

4 / Methods of Receiving Spiritual Guidance

SINCERITY OF purpose and clarity of need are ultimately the two most important variables to the guidance process. But there are also pragmatic factors, the practical steps one can follow in order to recognize spiritual direction.

This chapter will explore some of the specific techniques that have previously been alluded to. *All of the methods described in this chapter could be seen as ways of being alert for synchronicity.* Synchronicity is a precept of connectivity between the inner and outer world—a non-causal connecting principle—and we can understand experiences such as intuitive insights from meditation as well as psychic impressions from dreams as expressions of synchronicity touching our lives. We have no proven, cause-and-effect way of explaining these remarkable experiences which often convey profound guidance. And even though we can't force the issue, we can't make them happen, we can still invite them, be alert for them, and be carefully attentive when they arise.

We can use the principle of synchronicity as an umbrella concept for a wide variety of inspiration or even paranormal experiences. That is well within the scope of how a psychiatrist such as Jung or a spiritual philosopher such as Cayce saw the relationship between our inner and outer life. For example, Jung was fascinated with psychic phenomena and saw it as a manifestation of synchronicity. Cayce's teachings emphasize that the fundamental ordering principles of oneness, relationship and connectivity stand behind any dream, vision, or meditation experience by which our soul nature reveals itself.

Meditative Insight for Guidance

For many people the principle method for receiving guidance is the inspiration that comes during meditation. This is something we can do almost any time during the day, every day. The spiritual philosophy of Edgar Cayce contains frequent references to the way in which meditation can be a tool for guidance.

For example, he was asked by one person: "Is it possible to meditate and obtain needed information?" His answer: "On any subject! whether you are going digging for fishing worms or playing a concerto!" (1861-12) Apparently he meant that everything else fits somewhere between those two extremes in life—from the most down-to-earth pragmatic question to the most sublime problem of creativity. Meditation can be a valuable guidance tool anywhere along that continuum.

Someone else asked a question regarding the development of intuitive faculties with meditation. She wondered how she could best develop her intuitive ability. "By meditation" was Cayce's terse answer. The question-and-answer sequence continued, "And for what purpose should she use it?" Here Cayce emphasized that the intuitive, problem-solving skills that awaken with meditation should always be used in service to other people. "In developing herself and aiding others" was his exact answer. (803-1)

One kind of insight or inspiration that might come in meditation presents an interesting problem: situations in which you feel as if you are really getting guidance *for someone else*. When Cayce was asked what to do in such an instance, his advice was, "Be willing to share, but never force the issue." In other words, make an effort to communicate the information that may be for or about someone else, but never forget that you may have been wrong (i.e., it may really have nothing to do with that person). Don't force the issue. For example, upon hearing the account of your purported guidance, if the other person indicates an unwillingness to consider the accuracy of what you've said, then just drop the matter. "Never force the issue"—that's always a good rule of thumb.

One secret to meditating for guidance is to remember that meditation is a receptive state, a quieting of the conscious mind. It's an effort to put your attention on a focal point related to your spiritual ideal. Meditation is a matter of shifting your sense of identity from your familiar personality self (i.e., your everyday concerns and agenda) to your spiritual self or individuality. It's a matter of laying aside the personality self and awakening the individuality self.

The word or the phrase that you've chosen for your spiritual ideal could be a focal point for your attention during meditation. Or you could pick a favorite biblical verse, a positive affirmation, or mantra that's consistent with your spiritual ideal. It takes some practice keeping your attention single-mindedly on your chosen word or sentence. But with consistent, repeated efforts you'll learn how to begin to quiet down the agenda and the chattering of your conscious personality self. You'll learn to begin to be receptive and open to your higher mind and its guidance. In one of Cayce's most important teachings about meditation, he emphasizes that even in thirty to sixty seconds one can begin to make a reliable connection with the inner self. Even in half a minute—you can begin to make an attunement to the spirit within.

Let's consider more carefully how this would work in terms of getting guidance. Do *not* meditate upon the problem or the question itself. Instead, meditate first on your spiritual ideal or on your affirmation to get yourself connected to your wiser and more enlightened individuality. It may take thirty seconds, sixty seconds, five minutes, or half an hour.

At the end of this quiet time of focused attention, it's a good idea to have healing prayer for others and for world peace. And then at the end of your meditation time you would call to mind the question or the problem that you formulated earlier in the eight-step guidance process.

Pose the question inwardly, be silent, and listen for a response. What might you expect to receive? Here are several possibilities:

1. You may literally hear a still, small voice that comes to you as words—not words that other people in the room would hear if they were meditating with you, but inward words that may seem almost audible or words that are placed in your mind.

2. A new understanding or a new angle on the issue or on the problem comes to you. Many people who meditate for guidance experience this frequently. In

many ways this is similar to what happens in certain forms of dream guidance. Cayce suggests that in our dreams and in our meditations, often we move to a new perspective or a new state of consciousness from which we can look back at our problem with new eyes. And with that new angle, we can see more accurately what's going on. Simply having that new perspective allows us to deduce what ought to be done next to solve our problem. And so in meditation you may not so much get the direct answer, but you're able to see the problem in a fresh way so that you can later determine the answer.

3. As you're sitting silently in meditation holding the question, a third possibility is that you will get an insight about what has been an obstacle, what has kept you from finding a solution. As with #2 above, you're not getting the solution directly. Instead, you're being shown something that has to be dealt with so that later you can find the solution or the answer.

4. Some people during this silence period of meditation get a strong hunch or an intuition about exactly what to do in order to solve the problem. It may be a gut-level feeling or just a strong impulse about what would be right.

5. Remember that in the eight-step guidance process you will have made a tentative conscious decision. When you seek meditation guidance, the response may be feedback on that preliminary decision. You may get a feeling of rightness to confirm your tentative answer. Or you may get an unsettled or inharmonious feeling, warning you about that preliminary decision.

People experience this feedback process in meditation in different ways. Some people literally get a bodily feeling. Some get an impression or a sensation in a certain part of the body. It's different for each person, and it's a matter of practicing this to learn for yourself. In other words, from trial and error you learn for yourself the clues, or the cues, that tip you off to warning or to confirmation.

6. There's one other type of experience that may come as you sit in silent meditation, holding your question in mind. You may get nothing! You may just sit there, open and receptive, but no feeling, insight, or impression comes. In fact, for many experienced meditators that happens frequently. The only thing to do is try again. And it's a good idea to follow this meditative process multiple times, anyway, especially for important problems.

But if you continue to get no inner response in meditation, something may still be going on. Watch your dreams that night, be alert for synchronistic signs (including what's said to you during the day), and stay open to other forms of spiritual guidance that may come your way. It could well be that the attunement work that you did in meditation set the stage for spiritual guidance to flow into your life in a different form.

Give this process a try. A good place to start is with human relations. For example, consider a person that you're having trouble getting along with. Suppose it's a person at work, and you are this individual's supervisor. The question at hand concerns the fact that this person is up for a promotion. Making a tough decision like this has a context: you've already set a spiritual ideal for your life in general and you've set more specific ideals for your work life. The question you face is simply: Should I promote this person who works for me? You've collected all the facts. You've arrived at a tentative decision but you haven't told anybody yet, and you certainly haven't acted on it yet. First you want some meditative guidance to confirm your provisional decision or to warn against it.

The next step is to have a period for silent meditation. The initial five or ten minutes is exclusively for attunement. Then at the end of meditation you inwardly raise the question and see what comes. Perhaps it's a still, small voice that speaks to you, or a new consciousness about this particular situation, or a new awareness about an obstacle that needs to be overcome before you can clearly see what's best for this person and for the company. Or maybe you'll get a strong hunch or intuition about what to do. Or perhaps you'll just get a feeling of confirmation that your tentative decision is right or a feeling of something not quite being right about your preliminary decision. Or if you get nothing, you may simply want to stay alert for guidance to come in a different form later in the day or in the days ahead. In fact, this very practical and straightforward exercise for inviting guidance through meditation is something you can use for virtually any problem in life—from knowing where to dig for fishing worms to how to write a concerto, as Cayce playfully put it.

Dream Guidance

A second approach to spiritual guidance is working with dreams. We dream every night, and we're continually getting guidance from that source. If you're not remembering dreams every night, you're missing out on a great opportunity for practical direction.

But not only do guidance dreams come regularly and spontaneously, we can go about preparing ourselves to get a guidance dream. We can follow a procedure called dream incubation. It has sometimes been referred to as programming ourselves to get a guidance dream, and it involves following the preliminary steps already described: setting a spiritual ideal, articulating a question very carefully, doing our homework, collecting facts, having a tentative decision.

In fact, to prepare for dream guidance on a given night, you may want to review the results of these previous steps just before you go to bed. For example, you may even want to write in your journal about the issue or problem that you're dealing with and include a written statement of your tentative decision. Finally, just before going to sleep, you may want to come up with a one-line dream incubation request, something to have on your mind as you're falling asleep that night.

That one-liner can be a very powerful way to alert yourself to the synchronistic events that may come in your dreams—inner events that relate meaningfully to the difficulty or challenge in waking life. For example, your one-liner might be, "What shall I do next in this relationship?" Or, another night it might be, "What's the best career track for me?" or "What medicine do I really need to be taking to get well?"

Of course, it's not enough just to complete all these preparatory steps. One has to get to sleep, dream, and remember the experience. Then, it's very important the next morning that you be willing to *write down* anything that you remember, even if at first it doesn't seem to have to do with the problem at hand. For important questions, it's usually a good idea to follow this procedure over multiple nights. As we work with dreams in a *series* and begin to put together the pieces of the puzzle, the wisdom and the guidance may begin to emerge.

Dream *interpretation* is, of course, a critical part of the guidance equation. My own experience as a dream guidance workshop leader suggests that certain types of dreams are likely to occur when we've tried to prepare ourselves for inner direction. Knowing about these types of dreams can be very helpful for interpretation.

First of all, you may get a dream that simply gives you a new perspective on the current problem. There is no direct solution but it's a valuable chance to look at the issue from a different angle. Most people would prefer that their guidance dream would just give them the straightforward answer. But more often than not, the dream will give you a new way of looking at the current difficulty but will not immediately depict a solution. (A similar process can occur sometimes with meditation guidance, as already noted.) Your dreaming mind may simply stand aside, look back at the problem in an objective way, and show you a novel orientation for seeing the difficulty.

In counseling psychology this is called "reframing." For example, suppose you tell a problem to a psychologist, and she listens and then replies, "What I hear you saying is . . . " Without giving any advice or offering any solution, she proceeds to restate the problem or the difficulty from a little bit different angle. You might well listen to the problem being reframed and say, "Of course! When you put it that way, I can see that's what is going on." You then begin to recognize an effective solution, simply from being exposed to this reframing approach. Our dreams can do the same thing for us.

A second type of dream guidance is precognitive dreaming. Remember, you already have a preliminary decision that you've made and haven't yet acted on. The precognitive dream will show you what's likely to unfold in your life *if* you follow through on that provisional or preliminary decision. Based on what you see happening in the dream, you can decide: Is this the kind of outcome I want or not? It was only a dream—one that envisioned a likely future if you continued on the current pathway. But you still have the freedom to go back and change your course of action and change your decision.

The third frequent type of dream guidance is a direct solution, and this is the one we all want. Recall the personal example I described in chapter 3 concerning my move to Virginia Beach. It took two dreams for the message to get through, but a fairly direct solution was being offered. Of course, not all direct guidance dreams involve a dream character being so direct as to say, "Come on, move to Virginia Beach; I've got a job for you that begins Christmas." More often, this third type of dream guidance involves you the dreamer or some other dream character *acting out* a part of what needs to be done in waking life. In other words, you're shown an action that will lead to an answer or lead to a resolution of the problem.

A fourth type of frequent guidance dream seems at first to be off the point of the immediate problem or concern at hand. The dream speaks to *some other* problem or issue that has to be resolved first. Only when it has been resolved can your main issue really be dealt with. This is why sometimes, after having incubated a guidance dream, we seem to get something that has nothing to do with the question. Our soul self and our dreaming mind recognizes that something else needs to be done first, and once that's taken care of, then we can really deal with the primary concern. And we need to be willing to take the problem-solving in the sequence that our dream wisdom is showing us.

Of course, sometimes you may get no dream, even when you've prepared yourself carefully to get some guidance in the night. What if you wake up and you've got nothing? Suppose you sincerely tried to apply the dream incubation procedure and nothing came. Take heart in this principle: Your mind has been working creatively on your daily life issues all night long. Your mind is active, not just in those ninety minutes while you are dreaming, but all night long. The mind of the soul is always active.

So, here's a practical step you can follow when no dream comes to mind upon awakening. Lie or sit quietly, meditatively, and ask inwardly the question on which you incubated the dreaming process. Even though you don't remember a dream, trust that there has been soul

work going on during the night. As you ask inwardly—
and as you are open with a meditative frame of mind—
insight, inspiration, or an answer may come to you right
there in the waking state. You may not have a specific
dream to write down in your dream journal for interpretation. However, the intuitive insight that comes may be
just as valuable.

Finally, in our consideration of dream guidance, a
cautionary note is important. Sometimes we have
dreams that simply reflect our fears. Just because you
dream something does *not* mean it's precognition and
it's going to take place. If you can recognize that you fear
an outcome that's depicted in a dream, you should conclude that the message is ambiguous and very likely isn't
prophetic at all. It may simply be what Cayce called a
projection of the fear into the dream state. Until, through
prayer or counseling or meditation, you begin to release
and let go of that fear, you're not going to be able to rely
on a dream like that one because of the possibility that
it's only fear or anxiety produced. In a similar way, we
can have wish-fulfillment dreams. Just as a fear can create a dream, so can a desire. As much as we might like to
think that we are beyond Freudian wish-fulfillment
dreams, we all, from time to time, have dreams that
merely reflect our desires. In fact, this is why having set a
spiritual ideal is so critical. You need to be able to ask
yourself about possible dream guidance, "Is this merely
a reflection of my conscious desires?" And if the dream
is simply playing back to you something you want anyway, you can't necessarily take it as guidance from your
higher mind.

In my own experience, the best dream guidance that
I've ever received has sometimes included *some elements* of my desires but then *built upon it and stretched
me to something more* than I had consciously wanted. If
that element of surprise and stretching isn't in there, we

need to be very careful about assuming this is reliable spiritual direction to be followed.

Here's a reason why you may also find that working with a friend or a small group is very valuable for dream guidance. Sometimes other people working with you on dreams can provide the objectivity that's required for honest, safe interpretation.

Guidance from Professional Intuitives

Another way of working with spiritual guidance is to turn to professional advice-givers. This could, of course, include mental health professionals such as counselors and psychologists. But in this section, let's consider sources of guidance that aren't quite so traditional. In most communities there is a growing number of sincere, high-idealed people who offer their intuitive faculties to help clients find solutions to problems and questions.

How are we to understand psychic ability? As yet, parapsychologists have not been able to determine a testable, verifiable model to explain how the thoughts of one person could be received by someone else (telepathy), how an individual could have access to knowledge about a distant condition without the benefit of any sensory data (clairvoyance), or predict future events (precognition). The evidence that such experiences are possible, far beyond random chance occurrence, is nearly irrefutable. And yet, how is it to be explained?

Carl Jung prefers to view paranormal phenomena like these as manifestations of synchronicity. To his way of thinking, parapsychology was a descriptive science that could document extraordinary, synchronistic happenings but would always be frustrated in its attempts to find causes. If we adopt this point of view, a consideration of guidance that comes from someone else claiming to be a psychic is just another expression of synchronicity.

It is my opinion, based on more than twenty years of professional experience working with intuitives and talking to people who use their services, that often there is a valuable place for getting psychic input from someone else—especially when it's *one part* of a broader effort to receive guidance. That is to say, a psychic reading works best when it's in the context of working also with synchronistic influences of spiritual direction that may appear in one's own dreams, meditation experiences, signs, and outer events.

For those who want tips or recommendations on how to find the proper intuitive, I suggest that people go about looking for a professional psychic as they would any other professional person, whether it's a dentist or a plumber or a physician. Get references from other people. Check out sources, perhaps getting second opinions. That's just a common-sense way that we work with any type of professional service.

We should also be clear about what's reasonable to expect from a skilled psychic or intuitive counselor. That person doesn't have all your answers—maybe just some clues about how to more effectively find answers for yourself.

The point is well illustrated from a research study I conducted with a colleague, Dr. Henry Reed of Atlantic University in Virginia Beach. The research project was conducted over a two-year period—five week-long episodes in which we worked in-depth with fifty people at a time who were committed to finding guidance for important life issues. We led people through experiences with many different guidance modalities for their questions and problems. Psychic readings were part of that research project, along with all the other methods for obtaining spiritual guidance covered in this book.

After pooling the research data from all 250 participants, we arrived at several significant conclusions—
one of which was that getting multiple readings (that is,
at least two) was very important in order to make com-
parisons. With only one reading or one intuitive counseling session, a person is likely to feel vulnerable to
blind acceptance (e.g., "I guess that statement must be
true because a psychic told me"). Having two or more
readings which address the same set of questions put the
power of evaluation and judgment more readily back
with the seeker.

Another important conclusion concerned factors that
influence whether or not an individual is likely to get satisfactory results from consulting a psychic. It was interesting for us to note that the people who were happiest
with their psychic readings were the people who had
asked particular kinds of questions. In general, people
who asked the psychic questions which requested *further information* about the problem or difficulty were
more inclined to report a helpful encounter. This was in
contrast to people who chose to ask questions request-
ing the psychic to come up with direct answers.

This is a subtle but very important difference, and it
suggests that often the best results to be gotten from
psychics happen when we, the requesters of help, don't
surrender our free will or decision making to someone
else. Instead, by our attitudes and the types of questions
we pose, we can use psychics or intuitives simply as a
further source of gaining facts and information about
decisions we have to make. For example:

"What key talents should I keep in focus as I shape a
personal mission statement?" rather than "What am I
supposed to be doing with my life?"

"What factors, both internal and outer conditions in
the world, should I keep in mind as I make important
financial decisions next week?" rather than "What

should I do with my money?"

The validity of psychically derived information is an important matter. Another valuable byproduct of that research program was the creation of a list of criteria for evaluating psychic information. The items on the list came both from the researchers' insights and the feedback from the participants—that is, what they found to work best in their own experiences. Each of the ten can be posed as a question concerning the information received.

1. Does the psychic reading or the intuitive information have "*a ring of truth*" for you? "Ring of truth" means confirmable facts (material life realities that can be checked and validated) *and* it also means "feeling a tone of rightness" (something more subjective and personal).

2. Does the information give you *applicable things that you could be doing?* And when you put those things into application, what are the results? It ought to show benefits to yourself *and* to other people.

3. Does the psychic reading call you to the *best you know to be doing,* not merely something that's "acceptable" but falls short of your best?

4. Does the psychic reading *empower you* to take charge of your own life? It should be a red flag of warning if the psychic says, "Now come back in two months and I'll give you more information," rather than "Here's what you can be doing to be finding your own answers."

5. Does the psychic information leave you with a sense of *hope about your life?* There may be facts or may be insights in the reading that are hard to face up to—maybe even points of discouragement—but overall it should give you a sense of hope about your life.

6. Does the reading *speak your language?* Does it use words and metaphors and images that speak to you? That's indicative of the clairvoyant having tuned in to *your* soul.

7. What's the evaluation from a trusted friend? *Get a second opinion.* Let somebody else listen to the reading or read the transcript of the reading—perhaps only the parts of it you're comfortable sharing. Then carefully consider the evaluation of that person whose judgment you trust.

8. Does that reading *speak to unasked questions?* In other words, did the psychic tune in deeper than what you revealed by the nature of your stated questions? As a case in point, when Edgar Cayce was at his best, he answered questions that hadn't even been asked by the individual. They were deep soul concerns that had not been articulated on that list of questions submitted to Cayce.

9. Does the psychic reading *stretch you* to new and unconsidered parts of yourself, not just confirm things you already know? Reliable intuitives usually give information that goes beyond the status quo and really pushes you to grow.

10. Finally, does the psychic reading seem to *get better over time?* In the case of top-notch advice, as the weeks and the months and the years go by, and you look back at that reading, more and more will you appreciate the high quality of what you received.

Of course, all ten of these points are relevant to intuitive information that comes from *within yourself, as well.* However, many people have found that this list is especially helpful in an area where it's easy to feel vulnerable or worry that you may be gullible: evaluating the statements that come from a professional psychic.

Guidance from Inspirational Writing

One further method deserves attention as we consider the array of approaches to connecting with guidance. It's called inspirational writing, something that should be distinguished from automatic writing. Inspirational writing grows out of meditative attunement. It begins with an exploratory willingness to take paper and pencil and, after a period to center oneself, just begin to write about an issue or concern.

Cayce's spiritual psychology advocated this method, but clearly distinguished this safe, reliable method from a technique called automatic writing. For example, he was asked by a twenty-three-year-old university student, "Would a development of automatic writing establish a better contact with my Maker?" His answer: "For this body we would not give automatic writing as the channel. Rather the intuitional, or the meditation and then writing—*knowing* what is being written, if it's chosen to be inscribed in ink." (440-8)

With inspirational writing one is fully in control of the pencil. At its best, one has a sense that the ideas are *flowing through* the conscious mind, even though they feel as if they aren't coming directly from the conscious mind but instead are inspired from higher sources.

Most people who try to apply Cayce's suggestion have found that it works optimally if they begin to write about the issue or concern *immediately after* a period of meditation. It's *not* so much a matter of getting inspiration in meditation and then quickly writing it down. Instead, it's a process of making an attunement with the inner spirit and then just beginning to write. And if you don't know what to write first, you can just write, "Here I am sitting with my pencil and my paper and I'm going to write about ideas that come to me in regard to this problem that I have." And as inspiration comes to you while you're writing, you put it onto paper.

Of course, all this requires that your analytical mind take a break. You must put aside the logical aspect of the mind which is quick to want to evaluate whether or not the new thought or idea is worth writing down. But as you write inspirationally, everything's worth putting down—whatever comes to mind. You must say to your analytical mind, "Step aside for a few minutes; later you will get to come back and look at what's here on the paper and pick out the gems. In a little while, you'll be needed to separate the wheat from the chaff."

Not everything that gets written on paper during inspirational writing is going to be a brilliant insight from spirit, but you may find that as you are writing for five or ten minutes, there are a few moments of breakthrough as some fresh new way of understanding the issue emerges. It may not be the ultimate solution to the problem, but it could be significant little pieces or a clue for what you need next.

Inspirational writing is direct and, when it's done in conjunction with meditation, it is a very powerful tool for giving yourself a kind of psychic reading.

Applying the Methods for Receiving Guidance

The various approaches described in this chapter are not techniques to be used out of context or merely to satisfy curiosity. They are specific methods that you can actively pursue when you get to the fifth step of the eight-step guidance process outlined in chapter 3. Here again is the sequence:

1. Clarify your spiritual ideal.

2. Carefully formulate your question. Exactly what is it you want to know?

3. Collect the facts. Do your homework.

4. Arrive at a preliminary conscious decision that you could act on and still be in keeping with your ideal.

5. Seek guidance from outer sources and from inner ones.

6. Evaluate the guidance that comes to you.

7. Arrive at what you think is a guided decision, mak-

ing sure that it's consistent with your spiritual ideal. That guided decision may be the same decision you had at step four or it may be new.

8. Act on the decision, staying open for further guidance.

5 / Value-Directed Guidance

SPIRITUAL GUIDANCE requires more than just sound methods and reliable techniques. Its essence is a personal ideal, which is shaped by one's purpose and motive. In other words, the core value one has set for his or her life has a tremendous influence on the quality of guidance one *receives*, in addition to the powerful role that that central value or ideal plays in *evaluating* and *applying* the guidance.

An ideal is crucial to the guidance process because within oneself there are so many contradictory opinions and points of view, each clamoring to be the primary source of direction. Just think back to the last time you had to make a difficult decision. If you carefully watched your feelings, rational analysis, and intuitions about the matter, you may have felt as if you were fighting your way through a jungle of diverse options. You probably needed something like a sharp machete to cut through the tangle and see your way free to move ahead. A clearly articulated ideal is that tool.

Or consider another analogy. Sometimes a problem in life leaves us feeling as if we're in a fog, adrift on a turbulent ocean. In trying to deal with the problem, the fog symbolizes the many confusing options that come to mind. An ideal is like a beacon that shines brightly through the mist and indicates a path home. Through the many layers of the mind, an ideal serves like a lighthouse guiding a ship over stormy, foggy seas.

We all want our decisions and choices to be good ones; that's why we even consider the need for guidance—be it from a counselor, the I Ching, a dream, or any of the other avenues for getting direction. We want direction that bears good fruits—a more fulfilling and healthy life for ourselves *and* those around us. And that is what is most likely to come if we have formulated a clear and distinct sense of a personal spiritual ideal or core value.

A Model of Ideals in Spiritual Guidance

The Cayce philosophy of spiritual guidance includes a fascinating concept about dimensions of consciousness. Although this has often seemed complex and abstact to many people, the elegance and simplicity of this model of human consciousness shows us exactly why ideals are critical to spiritual guidance.

Consider first the notion that our normal, waking consciousness is three-dimensional. Our perception of reality is by and large focused on the physical world and our minds tend to understand things in terms of three measurements. For example, we see time as threefold: past, present, future. We see space as threefold, too: height, width, and depth. Modern physics *and* the teachings of mystics suggest that time and space may be much more complex than our everyday conscious minds think; but for the most part, three-dimensional consciousness serves us well day in and day out.

What is the next higher dimension? On this point, Cayce and Jung agree. It's the realm of ideas or thoughts.

> Best definition that ever may be given of fourth-dimension is an idea! Where will it project? Anywhere! Where does it arise from? Who knows! Where will it end? Who can tell! It is all inclusive! It has both length, breadth, height and depth—is without beginning and is without ending! Dependent upon that which it may feed for its sustenance, or it may pass into that much as a thought or an idea. Now this isn't ideal that's said! It's idea! see? 364-10

> If we wished to form a vivid picture of a non-spatial being of the fourth dimension, we should do well to take thought, as a being, for our model. (*Modern Man in Search of a Soul,* p. 184)

In other words, the mental realm has reality, which in many ways is just as genuine as the physical world (or maybe more so). As Cayce put it:

> For, thoughts are things! and they have their effect upon individuals, especially those that become supersensitive to outside influences! These are just as physical as sticking a pin in the hand! 386-2

At first it may take a little effort to appreciate the reality of this thought-form world. Where is a thought? What does it look like? How can it be real if you can't grasp or measure it? Consider this example: What makes this book you are reading real? Is it the weight of the paper and the color of the ink? That's a superficial way of looking at it. A more profound answer to this question says that it's the *ideas* in the book, ideas that come to life in your mind as you read. What's more, you can have the same idea which can be shared with any number of other people scattered throughout the world, and even throughout generations. An idea isn't limited to space *or* time.

Via the fourth dimension we discover the extraordinary power of the mind. We experience the amazing creative potential of our thinking—that we can literally create miracles by our thoughts (or, as one Cayce passage warns, we can also create serious crimes with our thinking). Fourth dimensionally we find that we are connected to each other. ESP works largely by this higher dimensional bridge from person to person. What's more, the fourth dimension is the source of the third. Over the years we have created a physical reality out of our attitudes, thoughts, and emotions. In this sense, the Cayce philosophy says that the third dimension is a projection of the fourth—that "Mind is the builder, and the physical is the result."

But the fourth dimension also has the potential to be a morass. It contains many different perspectives and options of human consciousness—many of them are expansive and liberating, but others are self-centered and ultimately unhealthy. One can easily get lost amidst the fascinating array of possibilities offered by the unconscious mind, and this becomes a critical issue whenever we try to engage inner tools for guidance, such as dreams, meditation, hypnosis, or psychic impressions. Something more is needed if we are to find our way reliably through all the possibilities. That something more is the next dimension.

The fifth dimension is an ideal. Whereas an idea (i.e., the fourth dimension) is the specific mental construct of an attitude, thought, or emotion, a fifth-dimensional ideal is the motive, purpose, or value that stands behind that fourth-dimensional idea. Remembering how the third dimension of physical reality can be understood as a projection coming from the next higher dimension (where "Mind is the builder"), a similar relationship exists between the fourth and fifth dimensions. An idea or thought or emotion is a projection of some underlying purpose, motive, value or ideal (i.e, the stuff of the fifth dimension).

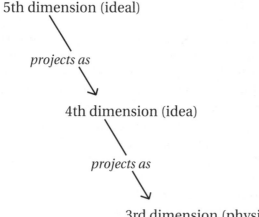

5th dimension (ideal)

projects as

4th dimension (idea)

projects as

3rd dimension (physical reality)

But what does all of this have to do with spiritual guidance? Simply that using the guidance tools that draw upon the fourth dimension isn't enough. Studying our dreams, listening for guidance in meditation, allowing synchronicity to work through the I Ching, or any other methodology still requires something that helps us sort through all the images, impressions, and feelings that come. This is where a personal spiritual ideal (the fifth dimension) plays such a helpful role.

Like a lighthouse beacon it moves us through the variety and complexities of the fourth dimension. And as it draws us through, we can pick up along the way the fourth-dimensional images, insights, and inspirations that we need, the ones that are consistent with that fifth-dimensional ideal we've set.

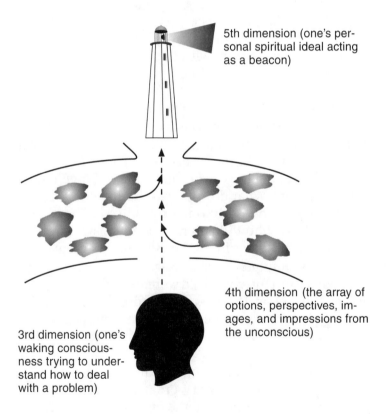

5th dimension (one's personal spiritual ideal acting as a beacon)

4th dimension (the array of options, perspectives, images, and impressions from the unconscious)

3rd dimension (one's waking consciousness trying to understand how to deal with a problem)

A Psychology of Ideals

As already suggested, in Cayce's spiritual psychology for receiving guidance, ideals are a frequent topic. Anyone who has studied the Cayce teachings knows the importance of motives, purposes, and ideals. For example, the approach to meditation advocated in this material is essentially ideals-centered. What's more, Cayce's elaborate theory of dream interpretation largely rests on the following assumption: the dreaming mind uses one's own ideals to shape dream experiences. In order to interpret many dreams we can ask what sort of ideal or motivation each key symbol represents. The dream as a whole can be addressed with the question, "What do I see about my life when I compare the action in my dream to what I hold as an ideal for my life?"

Cayce's pioneering work with natural healing methods and holistic health also rests on a foundation of ideals and motives for the patient. The person who wants to get well needs to have a sense of purpose for life. As Cayce often asked those who came to him for guidance about healing, "What do you want to do with your life and your healthy body once the ailment has been cured?" Those who didn't have a good answer weren't very likely candidates for his healing methodologies.

The most-quoted Cayce passage about ideals comes from advice to a forty-year-old woman working as a clerk during World War II. "Then, the more important, the most important experience of this or any individual entity is to first know what *is* the ideal—spiritually." (357-13)

Cayce described an essential human dilemma. Our minds—with extraordinary creative potential—are pulled in two directions. On the one hand is the attraction of an ideal, a positive, creative image of what is possible. In contrast there is the tug of material desires.

Unfortunately it's those limiting, destructive influences that frequently gain the upper hand.

How do those desires which are focused on materiality gain our attention? Usually it's either by (1) crises and emergencies or (2) good excuses and rationalizations. Think about your own life in those terms. What interrupts or diverts you; what interferes with the pursuit of your ideals? For most of us, it's an endless stream of material life demands that seem too important to ignore. In these stressful modern times, almost everyone has days that seem to be ruled by crises or emergencies.

The second attention diverter is a frequent impulse to say or do something that seems justifiable in the moment. In those instances, simply because we can rationalize it, we settle for something less than our best.

See if you can remember personal examples from the past twenty-four hours—instances in which diversions or detours took you away from your most deeply held values and your best self. This exercise isn't meant to make you feel guilty. It's merely a matter of seeing just how commonplace is the process that Cayce described.

Of course, merely recognizing this aspect of the psychology of ideals still leaves unanswered one vital question: "What is the best ideal for us to hold?" Clearly the Cayce philosophy has in mind a specific spiritual ideal as the *optimum:* the *universal* Christ. It was demonstrated and lived by Jesus. Just as significantly, it's a seed-like pattern in each one of us, no matter what faith tradition one may be following.

Of course, many people aren't ready to make a commitment to the "universal Christ Consciousness" (or even to similar wording to which they can better relate). For many individuals, that seems like too much to bite off, too big a stretch. Instead they would prefer to select an ideal that seems more within reach, although still demanding of them an effort to grow and change. Perhaps an ideal such as "loving kindness" or "peaceful centeredness" or "fairness" would be more appropriate for now. Later in this chapter we'll examine one way in which you can decide for yourself on the best spiritual ideal to which you can make a commitment. Perhaps you'll choose the optimal ideal Cayce encouraged, or you may select something that is a more modest stepping stone, eventually leading you to that optimum.

What happens in us when we make a commitment and invest ourselves in a personal spiritual ideal? The setting of a core value engages forces in the unconscious mind that can dramatically alter our lives. That's exactly why Cayce called it the most important experience that a soul can have.

But precisely what does it mean to "set a spiritual ideal"? Is it just a matter of telling someone else what you've done, or of writing it down on a piece of paper? Two crucial elements are central to the psychology of ideals. Both aspects play a role whereby the forces of soul, lying dormant in the unconscious mind, are stirred to life. Both involve an act of free will and an engagement of the creative mind.

Aspiration is the first ingredient in Cayce's psychology of ideals. To hold the universal Christ as a spiritual ideal means to aspire to its qualities. Maybe those qualities seem out of reach, but we can feel ourselves inwardly stretching and reaching for all that the Christ Consciousness means to us. The same would hold true for any other spiritual ideal chosen. What's most important to understanding the psychology of ideals is that the striving involves both the will and the creative side of the mind. We have to make the choice, and we need to use the imaginative forces to shape a relationship to that possibility for ourselves.

It probably comes as no surprise that "aspiration" is one of the two key ingredients in Cayce's view of how ideals work. Just think about how people use the word "ideal" in everyday language. It usually has the flavor of aspiration. For example, the ideal home situation is something that we can creatively imagine as the very best possible way of getting along with our family members. The ideal job is an imagined workplace situation that we long to have because all of our talents would be used.

Trust is the second ingredient in Cayce's psychology of ideals. This is a more subtle factor than aspiration. Think about how you might aspire to something but not trust that it's really alive within you, not trust that it's possible to experience for yourself. Without investing yourself through trust, you haven't yet set a spiritual ideal.

This may not be a point of view that's easy to swallow, simply because most of us find trusting to be very difficult. To trust requires a more challenging use of free will than does aspiration alone. Trust means a willingness to surrender and let go of fears and doubts. It means to place ultimate belief in forces beyond our personal, conscious selves. According to this perspective, you haven't yet set the universal Christ—or anything else—as your spiritual ideal until you let go and put your trust in it.

Think about a somewhat superficial example—one that allows a quick remembrance of what it feels like to trust. When you turn on a light, you trust that the electricity will be there, ready to light up the room. When you turn the handle on the faucet, you trust that the water will start flowing. In other words, you spend little of your day worrying about the availability of power and water. Now, of course, a critic could say that you're mindlessly taking it all for granted—that many people in the world don't have immediate access to these resources. But the point isn't how fortunate we are. These examples teach us something about trust—something that is related to trusting an ideal.

The authentic ideal you hold is the one you don't have to spend time thinking about or questioning. It has become so much a part of your life that it's a "given." When you meet a difficulty or a challenge, you know you can count on the inspiration and power of that ideal just as surely as you count on electricity and water when you need them. Some days your genuine ideal has the quality of being almost invisible to you because it's so deeply a part of how you look at the world. It's so essential that you don't stop to question it or worry about it. You can take it for granted.

Today's world at the turn of the millennium is an era that deeply needs a renewed vision of the power of ideals. Not pie-in-the-sky idealism. That too often fails to make the connection with practical life. What's so badly required in today's world is respect (even reverence) for that crucial step called "setting an ideal for one's own individual life." Cayce's spiritual psychology offers one very effective way to home in on exactly how to do it and make it work. Vivid aspiration is one key; the other is the courage to trust.

How to Set a Personal Spiritual Ideal

The best way to go about setting a spiritual ideal is to refer to our own peak spiritual experiences. These are moments in our lives—perhaps going back to childhood or early adult years—in which we caught a glimpse of a higher order of life. They are not intellectual abstract understandings about what our ideals ought to be. They are direct personal experiences, in which we caught a glimpse of God or the Truth or of a higher realm of life. We've all had these experiences. You would not be interested in the subject of spiritual guidance if you had not had some peak experiences. You may or may not have called them peak spiritual experiences at the time—

maybe just special moments. They are the unforgettable moments—for example, an extraordinary time out in nature, or a moment of love with someone, or a special dream, or a powerful prayer or meditation experience.

As an act of clear remembering you can bring back to mind two or three of these events from your past. But it's not just remembering what the experience was but actually *reliving* it. And as it begins to awaken certain feelings about life, you can just be open and be present to that sense of yourself and of your God and of the meaning of life. Finally, after a couple of minutes of reliving those peak spiritual experiences, you can invite a word or short phrase to come into your mind that describes that place in yourself. That word or phrase is a way of representing your spiritual ideal.

Of course, over the months and over the years, that word or that phrase may change as your experience deepens. But you are setting a spiritual ideal based on something you know is possible. Even though you may not be able to be in touch with it every hour of the day, you *know* it's possible because you've been there, at least a few times.

Here's a script that I use in my spiritual guidance workshops when we come to the point of setting an ideal. You can read this script into a tape recorder with your own voice (or have a friend make the tape for you), then listen to the tape meditatively and do the exercise. Each set of ellipsis points (. . .) indicates a pause of perhaps five seconds.

Sit comfortably now, I'm going to lead this brief exercise, and I want you to begin by closing your eyes with me and just observing the flowing in and flowing out of your breath. You don't need to try to change the rate or depth of your breathing. Just be present to this great rhythm of your body . . . And I want you to imagine a

timeline in which your whole life experience is before
you . . . back through yesterday . . . last week . . . last
month . . . your whole adult life is before you on this
timeline . . . your adolescence is there . . . your grade
school years . . . even your preschool years.

And as you lightly scan that timeline, I want you to
notice that just a few experiences stand out, with a certain luminosity to them—because these were peak spiritual moments in your life, when you caught a glimpse of
something different about life. These were very positive
moments, moments when you were in touch with life in
a more authentic and meaningful way than regular, daily
living . . .

I'd like you to remember and try to relive just two or
three of those special moments right now. . . [pause for
about sixty seconds]

And as you move back into the feelings of those moments, be still and allow a word or a phrase to come to
your mind that describes that place within yourself. . .
[pause for about twenty seconds]

And as you have that word or phrase now in mind, you
can begin to bring your attention back to your breathing
. . . to that great rhythm of your body . . . and let your
breathing bring your attention back to your sense of
physical presence here and now . . . And when you're
ready, you can open your eyes

Of course, having a word or phrase to describe your
spiritual ideal is really just the *beginning* of spiritual
guidance. No matter what quality, word, or phrase you
choose—love, or Christ Consciousness, or Buddha, or
oneness with the divine, or peace, or freedom—it should
describe a place in you which you *know is possible* because of your peak spiritual moments.

What's more, the spiritual ideal becomes a beacon to
your consciousness as you move into the myriad dimen-

sions of the soul mind. It designates the place from within yourself where you want the spiritual guidance to come. Remember that there are many different levels to the unconscious mind, each with the potential to offer its own perspective on your problem or issue. And not all those possible sources of inner guidance are going to be effective. For example, places of fear or self-doubt within your unconscious mind may offer up advice in the form of feelings, impressions, or dreams. But just because something comes from the unconscious doesn't necessarily mean that it leads to soul growth or success in the material world.

No, we've got to be more discerning when it comes to inner guidance, and focusing upon a spiritual ideal is the key. The ideal designates the level of consciousness from which we invite a guiding spirit to reveal itself. In addition, that spiritual ideal begins to serve as a standard or measuring rod against which you can evaluate information that comes from your dreams, or from psychics, or any other form of inner or outer guidance. Truly, without an ideal, we're like a ship without a rudder.

6 / I CHING

Carl Jung was not the first to recognize a non-causal ordering principle to the universe. Many ancient societies had oracles which relied on synchronicity. The best known in modern times is the I Ching or the Chinese book of change which is more than 3,000 years old. "I" (or Yi) in Chinese means "change," and "Ching" (or Jing) means "classic" or "a sacred book."

Hundreds of translations and adaptations of the I Ching exist, yet probably none has been able to capture adequately the authentic spirit and purpose of the original. Nevertheless, a version of the I Ching and its sixty-four thematic hexagrams—such as the one found in Part Two of this book—can be a helpful way to explore the principle of synchronicity.

Origins of the I Ching

The I Ching was created as a royal oracle for a Chinese dynasty three millennia ago. Ancient Taoists built a numerological system around the sixty-four hexagram patterns, becoming the dominant influence in Chinese folk culture of the time. It embodies wisdom—not the everyday wisdom of common sense but the wisdom of sages who understood the workings of cosmic forces. As a parallel to the Judeo-Christian tradition, one might look to Ecclesiastes or Proverbs in the Bible.

The essential philosophy underpinning the I Ching is that everything in the universe moves in cycles, no condition is static or unchanging. Change itself is a powerful force that governs the world and is the key to understanding cosmic events. In his book *Embracing Change: Postmodern Interpretations of the I Ching from a Christian Perspective*, Jung Young Lee writes that change "reflects the natural law that governs everything. Signifying the ultimate reality, change is analogous to the Christian idea of God." (p. 17)

The dynamic quality of all life is reflected in the yin (passive, yielding, nurturing) and yang (active, dominating, creative). The archetypal feminine and masculine provide a rhythmic pulse of energy and life that flows back and forth between these poles. This is far more than sexual attraction. More broadly, the I Ching teaches that one pole is always in the process of transforming itself back toward the other pole. For example, in the depths of despair, hope can be found. Or, at the height of success, one must be aware of the seeds of destruction.

The I Ching itself, however, has been subject to adoption and alteration over the centuries, most notably when the Confucians claimed it as their own. They read into its ambiguous, mysterious text their own moralistic interpretation. By the third century A.D., when Confucianism became the state creed of China, these embellishments became codified in an addition to the original I Ching—what was called the Ten Wings, referring to essays added on to the original text.

The I Ching was introduced to the West in 1923 with Richard Wilhelm's German translation. Wilhelm, translator of other ancient religious documents from the East such as the Tibetan Book of the Dead, was a friend and colleague of Carl Jung, who in turn began to make use of the I Ching in his psychological research. Jung began to use it personally and as a clinical tool to probe the unconscious with patients. Because he took seriously the claims that the I Ching was an oracle, Jung considered the casting of a hexagram to be an opportune occasion to observe the principle of synchronicity. The chosen hexagram could be seen as an essential part of the moment itself and provide a window of meaning into current conditions.

Jung's open-minded research efforts have stimulated countless other people in the last seventy years to explore the I Ching. Even though he is widely respected for his novel proposal of the Law of Synchronicity to explain the workings of the I Ching, the translation from which he worked has come under criticism. Decades after Wilhelm's death, as others with more sophisticated interpretive skills than he made their own translations, significant criticisms of the early twentieth-century work have arisen. For example, one critic (physicist and Chinese scholar Kerson Huang) claims, "This conscientious and painstaking work [of Wilhelm] represents a faithful rendition of the Confucian interpretation as seen through Christian eyes, and reveal little of the I Ching's original meaning."

In spite of limitations which may or may not exist in Westerners' attempts to understand the I Ching and to experience the synchronistic quality of its hexagram themes, this ancient book's philosophical foundation is universally applicable. The essential idea is that anything can be described in terms of only two basic elements. Every situation can be viewed as a sequence or string of yins and yangs.

But the complexity of modern life suggests that anything quite so simple is sure to fall far short of an adequate explanation of our problems and challenges. Think about how most any issue for which you would be likely to seek counsel and guidance seems terribly complicated and knotty. How could a teaching that reduces life to the interplay of yin and yang ever do justice to your life of diverse, competing demands? However, perhaps it is the elegant simplicity of the Taoist worldview that makes the I Ching such a powerful source of wisdom and direction for modern men and women. In a translation of the I Ching co-authored with his wife Rosemary, Kerson Huang writes eloquently of just how valuable this ancient book of changes can be to modern society. "As an oracle that explores the inner cosmology of human feelings, the I Ching is as valid as it was two thousand years ago. The only difference is that we know the distinction between the inner cosmos and the outer, and this, paradoxically, makes an oracle more necessary and acceptable." (p. 6)

The Hexagram Patterns

The I Ching consists of sixty-four patterns that can be created by a set of six lines. Each line represents one of two binary symbols:
- Yin (the universal feminine, passive, yielding, nurturing; depicted as a broken horizontal line), or
- Yang (the universal masculine, active, dominating, creative; depicted as a solid horizontal line).

Mathematically, sixty-four possible combinations can be created from a sequence of six numbers, each of which is either a zero or a one. The same holds true with the combination of yin and yang.

Each hexagram addresses a universal theme in the human condition, as understood by Taoist philosophy. As Jung Young Lee puts it, the sixty-four hexagrams "signify all possible patterns of changing process. These sixty-four patterns of changing process can best be understood as sixty-four archetypal or germinal situations of cosmic activity." (p. 18)

In fact, each hexagram is the product of a lower and an upper trigram (that is, a three-line arrangement). The eight possible trigram patterns correspond to the same number of essential forces in nature: heaven, earth, the depths (or water), thunder, mountain, fire (or sun), wind, and lake (or marsh). Each hexagram is therefore a combination of one trigram positioned above another one.

Associated with each hexagram is a Chinese script character plus a single word or a phrase to describe a focus to the oracle's message. Along with that titling of the hexagram is interpretive text. Anyone who has studied multiple versions of the I Ching knows that sources differ in how they title a given hexagram and the thrust of the interpretive text. In creating the version of the I Ching that appears as Part Two of this book, a synthesis of many scholars' efforts was attempted.

The interpretive text in full translations of the I Ching includes considerable material for the individual lines within a given hexagram. For example, hexagram #4, Youthful Ignorance, is created by this pattern of six lines:

In a comprehensive translation of the I Ching, there would be interpretive commentary for each of the six lines. One would study not only the opening text for the entire hexagram but also commentary related to certain lines (those which were cast as "moving lines," a concept to be explained below). The material contained in Part Two of this book confines itself to the opening text for the entire hexagram. For those who desire the more detailed approach with commentary on the individual line, one or more of the books listed in the bibliography may prove helpful.

How to Create a Hexagram

As you initiate your consultation with the I Ching, it is very important to approach the process with clear sincerity. The point of using the I Ching isn't to test its validity or to turn your decision-making responsibilities over to its influence. Instead, as you start the divination process with the I Ching, have a sense that it is a reflection of you, it is a way of exploring the best of human wisdom, just as you might consult scientific resources to help with a confusing problem. In spite of the similarity of the words, divination is not about the will of the Divine or the supernatural; it is about the depths of human wisdom. Consultation with the I Ching is self-prognostication, which means you are a participant and agent in what comes. You are the diviner, not the coins or the book, and any insincerity will lead only to self-deception.

If sincerity is such a key, we might well wonder under what circumstances we are most likely to shed mixed motives and be truly sincere, authentically one-pointed with our intentions. The answer no doubt is in situations of crisis, when the immediate demand for help is most acutely felt. It is in times of confusion and indecision that we experience a profound need for a wisdom beyond our own.

It is best to have a clear sense of the exact question. Perhaps you'll even want to write it down in your journal. Be creative with the wording. Get it just right. Make sure you've focused in before moving on.

Approach the I Ching with a plan to consult it only this one time on the matter at hand. In other words, refrain from any strategy to "do it again later if I don't get what I'm hoping for." To repeat the process for the same question shows insincerity and mistrust of the divination process. (But, of course, the I Ching may be only one of several methods used in seeking guidance on the problem.)

The mechanics of actually creating the hexagram offer two choices. Although there is a more deliberate and time-consuming approach with yarrow sticks, most people find that the coin method works fine. Select three coins for casting your hexagram. They should be of equal weight and size (e.g., three pennies or three dimes). The only other requirement of these coins is that they have a distinct "head" and a "tail" side, which is obvious if you're using familiar monetary coins.

When you throw the coins, you'll be counting up a numerical value based on heads and tails: heads = 3,   tails = 2.

You will throw the coins six times. After each throw, you'll compute the numerical value of the throw by counting up the heads and tails. Every throw will have a total count between "6" and "9"; in other words, the lowest count you could have would be three tails, a total of 6 points. The highest count would be three heads, a total of 9 points.

A hexagram is a six-part symbol constructed one piece at a time from the half-dozen consecutive coin tosses. For each throw you'll gather up the coins in your hand,

hold them meditatively for a moment, then toss them
onto a flat surface. Based on how the three turn up, you'll
draw either a solid or a broken line on a piece of paper.
(The "x" and "o" will be explained below.) If the total
number of the throw is an even number (i.e., 6 or 8),
you'll draw a broken line. If the total is an odd number
(i.e., 7 or 9), you'll draw a solid line.

9 = ——o—— old yang line (changes to yin)
8 = —— —— young yin line (unchanging)
7 = —————— young yang line (unchanging)
6 = ——x—— old yin line (changes to yang)

Notice the so-called "moving lines" or lines that have
a tendency to change into their opposite. For example,
the lowest score creates a broken line that is to be written down a special way. The little x in its middle is an
indication of its extreme nature (i.e., it was the product
of throwing three tails). In Taoist philosophy, anything
at one extreme is primed for transformation to its opposite; so, that yin line is mature (or "old"), on the verge of
transmuting to a yang line. The same process holds for
throwing all heads; 9 points makes a mature yang line
(with an o) ready to transform itself to a yin line. (More
about "moving lines" later.)

Build your hexagram *from the bottom up.* In other
words, the line determined by your second throw will be
drawn immediately above the line that you drew for the
first throw. The third line will be drawn above the second, and so on. When you've drawn six lines, determined
by your six throws of the coins, you've built a hexagram.

In order to find the corresponding commentary on
your hexagram, turn to the summary chart which appears on p. 241 of this book. To use the chart you'll need
to divide mentally your hexagram exactly in half. The
first three lines that you drew combine to make the lower

"trigram." The last three lines comprise the upper "trigram." Find your lower trigram along the lefthand margin of the chart, and locate your upper trigram along the top. Then, like a grid-finder, the two meet at one of the squares in the chart. The number in that square is the hexagram number you've just created by the coin tosses. Turn to the appropriate pages in the I Ching (Part Two of this book) to read, study, and reflect.

After reading, studying, and meditating upon the hexagram and its interpretive commentary, complete one further step if your original hexagram had one or more "moving lines" ripe to transform into their opposite. In other words, there is a *revealed hexagram* (the original one you determined) and usually a *hidden hexagram* (created by the transformation of those "moving lines"). Redraw the hexagram so that each "old yang line" (a 9) is changed to a yin line; and likewise, each "old yin line" (a 6) is changed to a yang line. The newly created hexagram—the one hidden in the current situation—is then a candidate for meditative consideration.

How to Use the Hexagram Obtained

The I Ching can be used as a source of divination and synchronistic guidance. Divination concerns both the unconscious and the spiritual dimensions of one's existence. By understanding more deeply the seedlike condition of one's life, it may be possible to see likely outcomes. In Jungian terms, divination is a matter of tapping the archetypal or germinal situation that may eventually mature and blossom. Lee says it this way: "Divination, as a part of human wisdom, is the art of intuitive thinking by which we search for a potential outcome to a particular stituation that can be applied to our personal and social life." (p. 19)

But fatalism isn't a basis of the I Ching. Free will is still there, as the Cayce philosophy emphasizes in regard to any sign or omen. Consulting the I Ching is in the context of our freedom to decide for or against an action. *The I Ching is simply a way of taking the pulse of current matters so that one can more effectively be involved in the dynamic, unfolding, free-will creation of life experience.*

More often than not, the seeker is able quickly to recognize some remarkable correspondence between the chosen hexagram and the challenging situation from daily life. In such a case, an element of direct guidance can be clearly seen, whether it is a course of action to follow or merely a frame of mind to adopt toward the problem.

However, the experience of many who have consulted the I Ching indicates that the relevance and meaning of a hexagram is sometimes not immediately evident. Any synchronistic link may be somewhat vague and may become evident only in the hours or days that follow. For this reason, it's crucial to approach any use of the I Ching with a measure of patience and willingness to tolerate ambiguity. Nothing is more likely to instill frustration than to come to the I Ching with expectations that it will be a magical answer book.

The version of the I Ching presented as Part Two of this book is actually a synthesis. The hexagram titles and interpretive texts derive from many different translations from scholars. The various interpretive texts are purposefully written with alternating masculine and feminine pronouns (e.g., the text for #1 is written with "he," but #2 is written with "she"). The sage or wise person described in many of the text passages is to be understood as either a man or woman. Some traditions have relied on exclusively the masculine pronoun, but here you will find an alternation from one to the other. *This is in no way meant to imply that some hexagrams are more relevant to one sex than to the other.*

The version of the I Ching for this book is unique in that it includes supportive parallel material from the Cayce readings. This is not to say that Edgar Cayce ever offered a translation of Taoist philosophy, although he was certainly a supporter of anyone's efforts to draw forth spiritual inspiration from Eastern teachings. What appears, however, as a supplement to each hexagram in this book is some of *the best of what the Cayce philosophy has to offer on those same sixty-four archetypal life themes.* As you study and apply the hexagram chosen by the coin toss, give equal consideration to the words of wisdom presented in Cayce's teaching.

Let's consider one example of how the process of using the I Ching might unfold. One man working with this synthesis of the I Ching and Cayce readings cast a hexagram at a crucial time in his career. After more than fifteen years at the educational institution where he worked, he felt as if his interest and commitment were waning. The new leadership at the top of the organization seemed to have a different ideal and work style than his own. Each month it was getting harder and harder to show up for work with any of the spirited enthusiasm he had once had. The problem wasn't helped by the fact that many, if not a majority, of his work colleagues felt the same way.

He turned to the I Ching in hopes of gaining an insight about his situation, and he cast with coin tosses the following hexagram, one that had two moving lines:

This arrangement, the earth trigram above the sun trigram (i.e., the opposite of the natural order), immediately augers something inauspicious. If the sun is beneath the earth, then surely the light is shrouded. In fact, the title for hexagram #36 is Perseverance in Darkness.

He read the text describing the overall themes of this hexagram, along with Cayce passages that dealt with persevering in the face of adversity. The text read:

> When circumstances prevent progress, even threatening one's ultimate continuation toward the goal, one does best to draw the light of her spiritual foundations within herself, to preserve it from harm. It is the warmth and constancy of this light which helps one to persevere in adversity, and to avoid the strong forces which attempt to turn her from her way.

Then he looked for ways to relate what he had just read to his situation. He took several minutes to consider meditatively how the I Ching text or Cayce passages might be linked to his current predicament. In this case, the synchronicity of the chosen hexagram was immediately evident. He felt as if he was in a situation of adversity, and the advice to draw the threatened light into oneself seemed wise. But how could he best do that? What practical steps could he follow to protect the light—i.e., his personal and professional ideal—from harm? In this case, the secondary hexagram—created from the transformation of the two moving lines—proved useful.

Both the third line from the bottom and the top line were cast as "moving lines" ripe for transformation into their opposite. As described above, the additional hexagram can be drawn by changing any line that was originally "moving" (i.e., a 6 or a 9) into its opposite.

Therefore, "moving yin lines" become yang lines; "moving yang lines" become yin lines. In this case, the alteration would result in this new hexagram, #27:

```
 ─────────

 ───   ───

 ───   ───
 ───   ───

 ───   ───

 ─────────
```

The title of hexagram #27 is True Nourishment, and it is accompanied by the following text:

> One's fundamental responsibility is to care for the body with right nourishment. True nourishment is that which furthers one's progress on the path. That which brings growth is what one should seek. What one ingests, be it food or thought, should not influence you to deviate from your goal.

He sat meditatively and considered the relevance of this message. He studied, too, the passages from the Cayce readings on this same theme. He saw two significant points. The first was literal. He recognized the need to improve his nutrition. The stress of the workplace disharmony was taking a toll on his body. Right eating was sure to help him protect his light.

Second, he saw a more symbolic application related to his daily thoughts and words. He needed to be on guard against his own discouraged thought patterns and his tendency to complain out loud about the problems. He was feeding his own soul by thoughts and spoken words, and he needed to make sure he found ways to truly nourish himself in this arena.

In the months that followed, things began to change. Initially it was within himself. He found a way to be more at peace with the situation. He found an inner determination not to let the attitudes or practices of the person at the top undermine his own sense of professional commitment. He recognized that he had invested too much of his own best self for too long to give up at this point.

Not long thereafter, a dramatic event took place: the senior management person in the institution decided to leave and was replaced by someone whose goals and approach were much more consistent with the entire staff.

Next Steps

You can begin immediately to use the I Ching as a way to experience synchronistic guidance. It is important, of course, that the process be engaged in with sincerity and a sense that the timing is right. The I Ching is hardly a tool to be used superficially or so often that it begins to lose any feeling of being special.

You might find it useful to consult the I Ching as one part of your search for guidance, as outlined in chapter 3: the eight-step approach. Synchronistic guidance from the I Ching can be a valuable part of step five, in which one searches for inner and outer indications.

You may also find it helpful to try a home-study research project in which consultation with the I Ching plays an important role. That personal experiment is described in the next chapter.

7 / Exploring Synchronicity and Guidance for Yourself

This concluding chapter of Part One invites you to a personal research project. It will not be a formal project in that no data will be collected and analyzed in a formal way, although the steps described *have* been used in a systematic study of synchronicity. At the end of the chapter, you'll find a brief report on the results from fifty-three people who carefully completed all aspects of this three-week project.

At your own pacing and in your own home, you can follow this research program. It's based on the hypothesis that one can sensitize himself or herself to synchronistic occurrences. Keep in mind that this is not an experiment to "make synchronicity happen" because that's not possible. As already noted in chapter 2—and worth restating here—the renowned Jungian scholar Dr.

Ira Progoff affirmed in his book *Jung, Synchronicity, and Human Destiny:* "By definition one cannot *cause* synchronistic events, but on the basis of observations in this area . . . it does seem possible to develop in a person an increased sensitivity to synchronistic events, and especially a capacity to harmonize one's life with such occurrences." (p. 132)

So, in the spirit of "increased sensitivity" you are invited to work on this three-week project. Most people find that it works best as three *consecutive* weeks, but if your schedule won't permit such continuity, it's possible to space the three segments. At the end of your personal project, you may find it instructive to "compare notes" with the experiences of others, which are reported in the last portion of this chapter.

Instructions for Week #1

Spend this week paying careful attention to (1) the outer events in your day and (2) the inner world of your thoughts, feelings, desires, etc. Look for coincidences. Watch for synchronistic connections between events, which cannot be explained through the law of cause and effect.

For example, you may think about someone whom you haven't seen for a long time. Then, out of the blue, that person will call on the phone or pay you a visit. Or someone may mention that friend in conversation, or maybe you will turn up a photograph of that person as you're looking for something else.

As another example, you may dream about turtles one night and the next day you will see a turtle on the road. Then later, someone may accuse you of withdrawing into your shell.

Keep a journal record of your experiences during the week. If you observe any synchronous connections during this week, jot them down. During Week #1 you are also invited to look for possible interpretations. But if none immediately occurs to you, that's okay, too. In Weeks #2 and #3 we will be more concerned with identifying the guidance that may be found in synchronistic events.

You might want to set up your journal entries in the following way. Make a column for recording the actual events—inner and outer. In a parallel column you can jot down notes about any interpretation or guidance you might see from the synchronicity. For example:

Synchronistic Events	My Feelings and Reactions
1. Dreamed of turtles 2. Saw turtle on side of road. 3. Friend said I live in a shell.	Maybe I need to be more open in my relations with people. Maybe these events are telling me that persistence is more important than speed.

Notice that there may be more than one interpretation to a synchronous experience. Feel free to brainstorm. Keep an open and playful attitude when looking for interpretations. If none occurs to you, just leave this column blank.

Record any and all experiences which seem to you synchronistic. You may discover synchronous events on every one of the seven days. However, it's just as likely that you'll only make entries on some of the days. Do keep in mind that synchronous events may easily extend beyond the limits of a single day. If, for example, you experience an event on day 4 that seems to be synchronistically related to an event on day 1, write your observation on the day that you recognize the connection.

You may, in fact, find no synchronous experiences during the week. If you don't have any, that's important information as well, in terms of this personal research project. You should still go on to Week #2.

Instructions for Week #2

During this week, you'll continue to look for synchronicity manifesting throughout your day. However, you'll add some new ingredients. First, you will hold in your mind a specific question and watch for synchronous experiences which may relate to that question. For the purposes of this personal research project, try using this question:

"What talent or side of myself can I develop more completely which will help me be more fulfilled in life?"

Feel free to reword this question in a way which will be most meaningful to you. However, retain the general focus of it. It concerns a desire to discover a talent or ability within you—yet one which you've not yet developed or perhaps not even recognized.

For example, one man who was seeking guidance on this question had a dream in which he was playing hide and seek with a group of children. He noted that although he was an adult in the dream, the age difference did not matter to the kids. Indeed, he felt as if he were completely one of the gang. The following evening, he turned on the television news in the middle of the broadcast, and the story in progress concerned the problems of teenagers trying to grow up in today's world. Then, later that week, he got a call from his church inviting him to be involved with its youth education program.

For him, the synchronistic message from these events was, "Develop that side of yourself which relates to youth and children." As a result of this guidance, the man got involved in the youth program at his church and later volunteered for the Big Brother program.

A widow who was also using this approach for the same question reported these events in her journal:

1) Uncovered my husband's old typewriter while cleaning out my closet.

2) Received letter in the mail from an old friend who was feeling lonely and forgotten.

3) Saw on television a report on the plight of elderly shut-ins—individuals who are unable to leave their homes without help.

As a result of these events, this woman felt herself led into a new activity. Although she could barely type, she started writing letters to shut-ins in her local community. This eventually evolved into a regular newsletter which provided humor, news, and needed information to individuals who were forced to stay in their homes because of disability.

A third example concerns a woman who noted on the same day two events which she felt were meaningfully related. First, she struck up a conversation with someone in line with her at the grocery store checkout. She discovered that this other woman's career was that of a music teacher. When she went home, she brought in the daily mail delivery. Among the "junk mail" advertisements was one from a local music store announcing a week-long sale on musical instruments. The two events, when reflected upon later, gave her the intuitive feeling that she was to bring music into her life more often. Not necessarily to take formal music lessons or buy an instrument; instead, it felt like an invitation to develop a latent talent in herself: to appreciate music. Perhaps that talent would enrich her life in some special way.

Throughout this second week, look for synchronous

events which may provide guidance in your search for new talents or abilities to develop. See if events coincide to steer you in a particular direction.

Along with this particular question-focused task, Week #2 of the research project also includes specific exercises. These exercises are designed to sharpen your sensitivity to synchronous events.

You're invited to select from the following exercises those that seem most effective for you. Try to use at least one exercise *each day* during this week, and note daily in your journal which ones you worked with.

Here are the exercises to choose among:

1) Listen meditatively to a "Synchronicity Awareness Reverie" sometime early in the day. You'll need to make a tape recording of the reverie, either with your own voice or, if you prefer, the voice of a friend. The wording for this creative imagery experience is written out for you as Script #1 in Appendix Two at the end of this book. Of course, feel free to adapt it or alter it, as you see fit.

Be sure that the script is read slowly as it is being recorded. This reverie should last about ten minutes. When you are ready to do this reverie, try to use it at the beginning of the day. It will then be easier to measure or track its effectiveness as you keep a journal record of your experiences throughout the rest of the day.

2) Take a random walk. In this exercise, you simply take a walk with no particular destination. As you take this walk, watch for signs which may have a bearing on your question.

The kinds of signs that you may see will depend upon where you go. If you pick a neighborhood to walk through, your signs may take the form of license plates, children playing, or street signs. If you choose a park for your walk, you may notice particular vegetation or wildlife which might carry symbolic meaning for you. Allow yourself to explore freely any interpretations of what you may see or hear during this exercise. For instance, if you see a crane flying south during your walk, you might ask yourself, "What does a crane mean to me? What does the direction south say to me symbolically?" After your walk, jot down these observations and thoughts in your journal.

3) *Explore a library.* This exercise is similar to exercise 2, except that you take your random walk through an available library. During your visit to the library, wander through the aisles and select books from the shelves at random. Leaf through them. See if words or subjects jump out at you which seem meaningfully related to your question or to other events of that day. Also stop at the magazine section or thumb through the card catalog.

The challenge in this exercise is to keep your mind "in neutral." You're not searching for anything specific. Rather, you're waiting for something to present itself which says to you, "I'm relevant to your question." If something does cause such a reaction in you, explore it further. See if it leads you to a new insight.

One man reported that it was through this very exercise that he discovered the work of Edgar Cayce, which has changed his life profoundly.

4) *Browse through a magazine or newspaper at home.* In this variation of the library walk, you simply thumb through an available publication and stay open to any articles, advertisements, pictures, etc., which seem to provide a hint of relevance to your question.

The key to making these exercises work is to watch for signs which seem to tie in to other events that occur spontaneously through the rest of your day. Also watch for items which may remind you of any recent dreams or dream images that were particularly impressive.

Record all your observations and thoughts in your journal. Once again, provide enough space for each day and a column to note which of the four exercises you carried out that day. You might want to set up your journal with columns for the exercise used, the synchronistic events, and any interpretive thoughts.

For example:

Exercise Used	Synchronous Events	My Feelings and Reactions
Day #1		
1. taped reverie	Met woman at grocery store who teaches music	Perhaps I should cultivate in some way an appreciation for music
2. browsed through ads	Saw advertisement for special sale on musical instruments	

Instructions for Week #3

During this final week of the project, you'll continue to use whatever exercises from Week #2 that seemed useful to you. However, you'll be using them to explore a new question. Here are three sample wordings of that same essential question, although you should phrase it in a way that is most meaningful to you:

"How am I doing on my spiritual path?"

"How well am I living up to my spiritual ideals?"
"What do I need to keep in mind to grow spiritually?"

This week will also make use of a new tool in the study
of synchronicity: an adaptation of the I Ching which appears as the second half of this book. Carl Jung, for one,
found the I Ching to be a valuable approach to experiencing synchronicity. This adaptation uses the sixty-four
traditional hexagrams and their themes but adds wisdom from the Cayce readings as a parallel source of inspiration and insight.

Be sure you've read and understand the approach for
consulting the I Ching which appears in chapter 6. Once
again, you'll be using your journal as a place to keep a
record of your experiences. Here are the steps you'll be
following at least once, and perhaps several times, during Week #3:

1) Clarify your question. It's very important to have a
clear sense of your question. Make it your version of the
spiritual-growth question described above (e.g., "How
am I doing on my spiritual path?"). Write it down in your
journal. Play with the wording. Get it just right. Make
sure you've done this before moving on to step 2.

2) Consult the I Ching on day 1. During this third week
of the personal research project, you'll work with the I
Ching on day 1 and day 7.

On day 1 pick a half-hour when you won't be disturbed
and sit comfortably in a quiet room. Place the book,
coins, and a pad and pencil near you.

Before actually throwing the coins, prepare your mind
by listening to the guided reverie that you can make from
Script #2 in Appendix Two of this book. This guided imagery experience will take on an imaginary journey
where you will consult with a wise counselor. It sets a

mood for working with the I Ching.

Immediately after the preparatory reverie, open your eyes and proceed to throw the coins, constructing your hexagram as you do. Recall from chapter 6 that we'll be using this formula: Count a numerical value based on heads and tails, where heads = 3 and tails = 2. You will throw the coins six times. After each throw, you'll compute the numerical value of the throw by counting up the heads and tails. Every throw will have a total count between "6" and "9"; in other words, the lowest count you could have would be three tails, a total of 6 points. The highest count would be three heads, a total of 9 points.

A hexagram is a six-part symbol constructed one piece at a time *from the bottom up.* For every throw of the coins, you'll draw either a type of solid line or a type of broken line. Use this formula, as it was described in chapter 6, for translating the points of the coin throw into a specific type of line:

9 = ——o—— old yang line (changes to yin)
8 = —— —— young yin line (unchanging)
7 = ———————— young yang line (unchanging)
6 = —— x —— old yin line (changes to yang)

Then use the chart on page 241 to help you find the number of the hexagram you've created. That chart involves matching the lower trigram (i.e., the bottom three lines) with the upper trigram. If you have any changing lines in your hexagram (i.e., a 9 or a 6) calculate that additional hexagram that your situation may be transforming itself into.

Take three to five minutes to think about what you read in the I Ching concerning your specific hexagram (and perhaps the secondary hexagram created by the changing line). Try at least these two approaches as you

have a time for reflection and interpretation:
- When I consider my problem or issue from the point of view of the opening teaching of the hexagram, what insight does it provide?
- When I read the parallel passages of wisdom from the Cayce readings, do any of those excerpts seem to speak directly to me and my situation?

During this initial three to five minutes of reflection you may or may not gain a sense of guiding direction. If you do recognize connections or useful guidance, immediately make notes in your journal worksheet, including the hexagram number and your reactions or impressions. If insights come later in the day, write them down as soon as it's practical to do so.

The next phase is equally important. During days 2, 3, 4, 5, and 6 of the week, be open and alert to experiences that seem to tie in to the section you read from the I Ching. In other words, do any coincidences happen that relate to your hexagram message? Keep a journal record of anything that seems relevant.

Finally, on day 7, consult the I Ching again. Follow the same format as before; ask the same question. If you found it helpful to set a proper mood or tone, once again use the preparatory reverie tape from Script #2. Then proceed to throw the coins and make your hexagram.

Probably you'll get a different one than you had on day 1, but of course it is possible to get the same one.

Once again, you'll want to take three to five minutes to think about what you read in the section for this hexagram. Record your thoughts and reactions in your journal, including your comments about whether you feel this session with the I Ching seems to tie in with your consultation on day 1. If so, how?

By the end of Week #3 you may feel that you're now ready to make a decision about your situation, even if it's just to commit to a new frame of mind about the problem.

We hope that the exercises from these three experimental weeks have made you feel more comfortable working with the I Ching, and you'll be ready in the future to make use of this tool for experiencing synchronicity.

Results from the Synchronicity Research Project

In one offering of this research protocol to interested parties, my colleague Chris Fazel and I collected detailed reports from fifty-three people who completed all phases of the project in their own home environment. The information on their report forms provided interesting statistical data. Much of this information would probably correspond with your own personal experiences. For example, have you ever found that synchronous experiences seem to be more frequent or pronounced if you've been meditating regularly? According to the information sent back to us, regular meditation seems to have a positive effect on both experiencing synchronicity and finding guidance through it.

Also, there is a definite correlation between dream recall and experience of synchronicity. Those who were successful in finding clear guidance through synchronous events remembered an average of four-and-a-half dreams per week. (This number isn't limited to just the research period; rather it's a self-reported, long-term average.) Those who received only marginal guidance remembered an average of three-and-a-half dreams a week, and the relatively few people who reported finding no guidance at all through synchronicity remembered just over two dreams a week.

This correlation would indicate that one way to encourage synchronous activity in your life may be to work more conscientiously with your dreams. Indeed, many of the participants described synchronous experiences which related directly to specific dreams.

Of course, the central question to address is this: "How many research participants overall were successful in getting guidance to a question by observing and interpreting synchronous events?" Of the fifty-three reports studied, twenty-seven (or 51 percent) said they were successful in getting clear guidance to a specific question with this method. Thirty-four percent said they weren't sure yet, but perhaps guidance would become clearer later. Only eight of the fifty-three (or 15 percent) said they were unable to find any guidance at all through synchronous experiences.

Distinctions of gender, age, or years of experience in paranormal studies seemed to have no bearing on whether or not participants were successful in getting guidance through synchronicity. The only other factor which did seem to influence the success rate was the level of observed synchronistic activity *before* this project started. In other words, if individuals had already experienced synchronicity on a regular basis in the past, they were more likely to find guidance with it during the research project. This isn't a surprising discovery and probably indicates simply that it takes practice to cultivate the skill of observing synchronicity.

Although 15 percent of the returns reported no success in finding *guidance* through synchronicity, all except one reported success in *observing* the phenomenon at some time during the project.

There were many classic examples of synchronicity, such as thinking or speaking about someone only to have that person call or appear a short time later. Several participants told of opening a book or magazine at random and reading something that related directly to other events in their day. Sometimes these experiences seemed to provide an element of guidance. At other times they just seemed to tie in mysteriously with the person's thoughts.

This would indicate that we can divide examples of synchronicity into two categories: those that carry an aspect of guidance and those that don't. Of course, the division between these two categories is a fuzzy one. Guidance in a synchronous experience may not be evident until quite some time after the event. Also, the amount of guidance found in any experience depends largely on the attitude of the individual. Yet, putting these considerations aside, it seems that the purpose of some synchronous events is simply to awaken us to the oneness of life.

For example, one woman reported this coincidence: "My husband and I listened to the taped reverie [provided in the materials for this project]. It was time for dinner and we prepared shrimp. I wondered if shrimp and oysters were animals and, if so, what was their mode of reproduction. We looked in an encyclopedia and discovered that they were oviparous, meaning they lay eggs. We finished our dinner and tuned in by chance to a TV documentary on oyster breeding!" She was amazed at this coincidence and decided that it was indeed synchronous. Yet, at first she was unable to find any guidance in it. For this coincidence to be an example of synchronicity, there must be a *meaningful* relationship to these events even if no clear guidance is evident. Upon further consideration, the woman found meaning in the guise of a pun. Her question during this phase of the research project had been, "What new talents can I develop to further my spiritual growth?" She extrapolated from her synchronous experience that "there is a 'sea' of opportunities just waiting to 'hatch.'"

Now the question that naturally arises is, "Was there really a meaning behind that coincidence or did she invent a meaning for it?" That question is ultimately unanswerable, which simply highlights the difficulty in proving or disproving the law of a "meaningful coincidence." Meaning is a highly personal matter.

However, for others, the direct guidance content in their synchronous experience was far clearer and more dramatic. One man reported an unusually high number of electrical difficulties throughout the research period. During the three weeks of the project, he had electrical problems with a tape recorder, a camera, a car, a lamp, and even his apartment. These coincidences alone seemed meaningful to him, but when he used the I Ching, he was really surprised. Through the random tossing of coins, he was led to a hexagram involved with the use of power. In reporting his interpretation, the man wrote, "I must learn to use my innate powers correctly (i.e., switch them on) to improve my spiritual life and keep moving forward."

One of the most interesting aspects of this research study was the array of letters and notes that accompanied participants' reports. Most of those involved were like this man from New Zealand who already had considerable experience with synchronicity. He wrote:

"For many years I have observed a great deal of synchronicity in my inner and outer life. Happenings such as:

• Prophetic dreams which act out at a later date;
• Receiving a very strong visual impression or thought of a person within minutes of that individual entering the door or telephoning;
• Having a financial boost prior to needing extra money for some matter;
• Planetary transits [i.e., astrological] to my birth chart coinciding with incidents and health changes;

- Opening books at 'just the right page' for 'just the right quote or information' when researching material for my writing; and so on . . . "

Many of the participants had remarkable instances of synchronicity during the experiment. Sometimes they were simply occurrences of synchronicity without any specific guidance; other experiences seem to present a spiritual lesson or reinforce faith in higher forces. Here are ten additional examples:

Case #1: The horse trainer.   In this account the inner dilemma of a hiring decision is matched by outer events which have a play-on-words. "I went to a horse trainer's ranch to watch her ride some horses. I was thinking of hiring her to train a colt for me, but I had to watch her ride first to be sure she was right. As she was getting ready to saddle up—on a beautiful, sunny day in the middle of a severe drought—a thunderstorm blew over with too much lightning to be outdoors. It rained so hard and got so muddy that there was no way she could school horses that day. The footing was too slick. So I went home without hiring her. Two days later I found out that she would not have been suitable for reasons other than her riding skills. The storm saved me from making a very big mistake. It literally "rained on her parade" and told me that my idea to hire this person was "all wet."

Case #2: The crossword puzzle.   In this very brief anecdote, inner questions and outer events remarkably coincide. "I was doing a crossword puzzle, and I was stumped on two clues. I put it down and turned on the TV. In a few minutes of television, they answered both of my puzzle clues."

Case #3: The calendar quote.   This account, like the

one above, has a remarkable synchronistic match coming from the media. In this case the coincidence served to draw her attention to an important principle about life. "I'm changing the date on a page-a-day calendar. There's a quotation from Simone de Beauvoir, 'One's life has value so long as one attributes value to the life of others, by means of love, friendship, indignation, and compassion.' Under it is this statement: We are, after all, a human family. At that exact second the song 'We Are Family' came on the radio! I haven't heard this song in years. I wasn't even listening to the station I usually would. If this hadn't happened, I wouldn't have paid any particular attention to the quotation."

Case #4: Timely money.   This story has a surprising match, to the exact dollar, between a need and some unexpected income. "I received in the mail a membership application for the Institute of Noetic Sciences. I was particularly drawn to it but felt I couldn't afford it at this time. The least expensive fee was $35. As I continued to open my mail, there was a letter from a friend containing a check for $35 as repayment for a long-forgotten loan of $10."

Case #5: A recurrent parable image.   Using two of the exercises for the research project, this person has multiple encounters with a biblical parable. "The parable of the seed was mentioned twice in my presence, and once I heard it on TV. My hexagram commentary referred to sowing seeds. I took the random walk through the library and a book fell open to a story about the parable of the sower and the seed."

Some participants were particularly successful at experiencing synchronicity through dreams.

Case #6: Dream synchronicity with a son. "I had a very vivid, frightening dream about my four-year-old son in trouble in a large body of water. I tried to help but was unable. I had been concerned about leaving the church and how that would affect his religious training. The next day he came home from pre-school with a picture and explained to me he was drowning in the ocean and some men were helping him. I [had] not discussed this dream with anyone."

Case #7: Dream synchronicity concerning illness. "I had a dream about a precise illness happening to me but it was cured according to the physician. The next day a friend of mine called from Paris (she calls twice a year) and said her illness had gone away. It was at the same place on her body as it had been on my body in the dream."

Sometimes synchronistic occurrences were linked to psychic or paranormal events. Here are three examples submitted from the research project:

Case #8: Synchronistic help arrives. "I was feeling frustrated with my current life circumstances and began praying while driving home, asking for help in replacing my negative responses with joy. When I got home, I had a phone message from a massage therapist I hadn't spoken with in months and who has never called to just chat. When I returned her call, she told me she wanted to give me some spiritual literature (including a box of old *Venture Inward* magazines). She and I talked about releasing fears and opening to change—the very issues I was struggling with."

Case #9: A friend in need. Although one might say that the following story was simply a case of telepathy that was continually ignored, Jung felt that such paranormal occurrences were manifestations of the synchronistic principle. "A good friend of mine kept coming into my thoughts from day 1 to day 5 [of the first experimental week]. On day 5 he called me and told me that he was going to have outpatient surgery the next day. I felt guilty. When a person comes to my mind that way, there is usually always a reason. I felt badly that I had not listened to my feelings and called him, but I had waited until he called me."

Case #10: A medical emergency. "I woke up early and had an unusual impulse to hurry and go to work one hour earlier than planned. There was an accident on the freeway right in front. People were hurt. I took the first exit and found a police squad car stopped for breakfast. They were able to assist. The feeling of urgency was gone after I left the police, and it was replaced with a feeling of warmth."

Conclusions

This project and similar experiments with synchronicity are ongoing. More and more frequently the topic is becoming a focal point for master's theses and Ph.D. dissertations. Although the subject will always remain somewhat mysterious and elusive—that's the very nature of something non-causal and outside the realm of manipulatable variables—we can learn more about *how it works in people's lives.*

Just as astronomy and meteorology are *descriptive* sciences, so too is the science of synchronicity investigation. We can't cause a comet to appear or a hurricane to form, any more than we can create a synchronistic moment. But we *can* study all three and come to understand more fully their marvelous existence. I hope that this book, and especially the kind of personal research project described in this chapter, will stimulate you to start paying more attention to synchronicity and its potential as a potent guiding influence in your life.

Part 2

The I Ching with Wisdom
from the Cayce Philosophy

I CHING

[BOOK OF CHANGE]

WITH PARALLEL WISDOM FROM THE EDGAR CAYCE READINGS

Then, the destiny of the soul—as of all creation—is to be one with Him; continually growing, growing, for that association. What seeth man in nature? What seeth man in those influences that he becomes aware of? Change, ever; change, ever. Man hath termed this evolution, growth, life itself; but it continues to enter. That force, that power which manifests itself in separating—or as separate forces and influences in the earth, continues to enter; and then change; continuing to pour in and out. From whence came it? Whither does it go when it returns? 262-88

1 / Creative Initiative

The embodiment of all that is strong, creative, and forward moving—pure yang—the masculine. This creative impulse is constant—flowing through our lives and our world. It is the essence of all things—perpetual regeneration without waste. From this cosmic example, one can model his inner self, aspiring to creative initiative and consistency of movements in the flow of cosmic unity. It is with this ceaseless power of heaven that the goal is realized.

(Q) How may I gain more initiative?

(A) By depending more on Him and less on self. This is not contradictory, though it sounds so until one puts it to the test. Walk with Him often and He will ever give thee initiative. 2746-2

(Q) Can suggestions be made as to how self-mastery can be developed; that is, willpower and initiative?

(A) Study that from the spiritual angle, if there would be that power, that might to succeed. For, as has been given, all first finds concept in the spiritual. The mental is the builder. This is true in planning the life, the relationships, and every phase of man's existence or experience. 2322-2

Remember, the Lord thy God is *One!* Thy experiences through the earth then are one. The activities of thy body, thy mind, thy soul *should* be then as one. And each experience to thine self comes as those influences that make for regeneration, uplift, the experience which if taken into the activities of self becomes as the means for bringing harmony and peace in the inner self.   1183-1

Those then that are come into the new life, the new understanding, the new regeneration, there *is* then the new Jerusalem . . . the place is not as a place alone but as a condition, as an experience of the soul.

Jerusalem has figuratively, symbolically, meant the holy place, the holy city—for there the ark of the covenant, the ark of the covenant in the minds, the hearts, the understandings, the comprehensions of those who have put away earthly desires and become as the *new* purposes in their experience, become the new Jerusalem, the new undertakings, the new desires.   281-37

. . . for whether there is, as is given, the ascending into the heavens to bring down that as would be understood, or the descending into the depths to bring up as to that that would be heard, or going beyond the seas to bring over that as has been studied or seen, or visioned by others, that as was given *still* is the same: That lies within each entity, that awakens to the spirit of truth, or the essence of regeneration in the spirit of truth, that makes for the continuity, or the active forces in the spirit of life, or the essence of same itself.   294-140

As the carnal foods make for strength, physical vitality, so do the foods of the spirit make for *strength* in the Lord . . .   274-3

2 / Responsive Receptivity

If one is to be in touch with the cosmic flow, she must develop a consciousness that will permit communication. A responsive relationship with the One is required. Yielding and open, the forces of heaven can penetrate into the depths of the mind. Through the wide gate of her spirit's awareness, the sage receives the earth-intended force and humbly puts it to use for all people. This is pure yin—the feminine—and a sign of peaceful involvement with life.

And the centers becoming attuned to the vibrations of the bodily force, these give a vision of that as may be to the entity an outlet for the self-expressions, in the beauties and the harmonies and the activities that become, in their last analysis; just being patient, long-suffering, gentle, kind. *These* are the fruits of the spirit of truth; just as hates, malice and the like become in their growths those destructive forces in creating, in making for those things that are as but tares, confusions, dissensions in the experiences of an entity.

Those then are the purposes of the entrance of an entity into a material plane; to choose that which is its ideal.   987-4

Only those become conscious of same that have attuned themselves to that which is in accord, or seeking to know—then—His will; for each soul, every soul, should seek to attune its mind, its soul—yea, its body-vibrations—to that He, the Son of man, the Mother-God in Jesus the Christ, lived in the earth. Tune in to that light, and it becomes *beautiful;* in that you think, that you are, that you live!   254-68

But know that each soul, even self, would have learned much more keeping close to nature. And kicking a clod may be a very uncomely thing to some, but you are closer to Mother Earth and God in same than listening to many an individual rant on what others should do!

257-253

For each and every individual should own sufficient of the earth to be self-sustaining. For the earth is the mother of all; just as God is the Father in the spiritual, the earth is the mother in the material. These are the supplies, the sources, from which individuals sustain or gain the sustenance for the material undertakings.

470-35

So may one be joyous, being kind, being loving, being open-hearted, open-minded to those things wherein that in the word spoken, in the manifestation of the smile in the face, in the eye, to those that the self contacts, there is brought forth that from the hearts, the minds, the souls of those whom the entity contacts day by day!

Turn self *inward* then, at given periods, at specific times.

274-3

Unless you become as open-minded, unless you can get mad and fight and then forgive and forget. For it is the nature of man to fight, while it is the nature of God to forgive.

3395-3

3 / Proper Beginnings

It is the time to begin. Like a plant struggling out of the earth, the strength required is not yet equal to the powerful external forces. It is natural for there to be some confusion as one prepares to begin. But to start alone would be disastrous. Assistance is required, and to attract this help one must show receptivity and even humility. Force, arrogance, independent action bring ruin. In this sweeping aside of the ego, this recognition of one's own limitations, lies the perspective required to transform chaos into the beginnings of the path. Perseverence will be required.

(Q) How may the body-mind make the greatest material advancement in the next twelve months?

(A) . . . Study to show self approved unto that, whatever has been set, or whatever may be set, as the ideal. Set the ideal above those things that are manmade, or of carnal influence. Let the fruits of the spirit (which is Life itself) be the ruling influence. 282-4

But take time to add something to your mind mentally and spiritually. And take time to play a while with others. There are children growing. Have you added anything constructive to any child's life? You'll not be in heaven if you're not leaning on the arm of someone you have helped. You have little hope of getting there unless you do help someone else. 3352-1

(Q) Give specific directions for approaching this study of music under present conditions.

(A) As has been given all along here, again and again—

see the rhythm in the activities of every nature; whether in viewing the scrubwoman or the artist in giving expression—see the timing of same necessary to make the activity *valuable* and of a *spiritual* nature in its essence!

949-13

Find thy ideal—spiritually, mentally, materially. Know in *whom* ye believe as well as in what. Know that He, the Ideal, *has* been, is, manifested in the earth from the beginning of time, and that His promises are *thine*—if ye will embrace them.

2397-1

. . . as the spirit builds, as the spirit forms in its activity in mind, the mind becomes then the builder. The mind is not the spirit, it is a companion to the spirit; it builds a pattern. And this is the beginning of how self may raise that expectancy of its period of activity in the earth. And this is the beginning of thy ideal. Of what? Of that the soul should, does, will, can, must, accomplish in this experience!

2533-6

(Q) When did I first exist as a separate entity?

(A) Would this add to thy knowledge? The first existence, of course, was in the *mind* of the Creator, as all souls became a part of the creation. As to time, this would be in the beginning. When was the beginning? First consciousness! There is no time, there is no space. Hence the injunction, first know thy spiritual purposes. Ye know thy ideal.

2925-1

4 / Youthful Ignorance

Beginnings are fraught with doubt and indecision. In spite of any ignorant errors, one still moves ahead. Inexperience and innocence need not prevent ultimate success. A childlike way that is free of any guile can even lead to a beginner's luck. It is the internal framework that needs ordering and learning.

Follow that way that gives the understanding to the youth, for, as has been given, "In youth seek the Lord, and when thou art old thou will not depart from Him," for in Him is life, and the light is the light of the world, for seeking Him, having Him in the heart and the mind, all else will be added unto thee, for the world and that therein is His, and to be one with Him is to be the colaborer with the Creator. To be otherwise is to set self in that position of being at-variance with Him.   4714-1

One that finds childhood, especially the adolescent age, the most interesting to the body, both from the mental standpoint and from the spiritual essence as may be manifested in the hopefulness, the genuineness, the sincerity, of youth in its endeavors.   5424-1

(Q) Any message to the group as a whole?
(A) Be thou *strong* in thy might in thy youth, that when the evil days come they will not be as troubled waters but that ye may save those who are weak.   792-1

If same is founded in love, in peace, these beget the children thereof. These must be considered first and foremost in the heart of each as they approach a truth as may be founded, even in that termed by the world as superstition, ignorance, and such; yet out of the mysteries to the blind comes those forces, those manifestations, that make life worth living for those that seek to know the light.   254-52

Do not jump at conclusions. Analyze *all* relationships. Hold no grudges, no feelings, because others have not applied or do not apply that as ye feel to be right, or ye feel should be. Suppose self in the other individual's place, and hold thy tongue from speaking guile or evil of anyone.   2074-1

(Q) [993]: Would appreciate guidance at this time regarding healing group and how I may best improve same.
(A) Let thy self be lost wholly in that thou givest of thy time, of thy self, of thy mind, in thy service to thy fellow man. Be patient; be kind; be gentle; be forgiving, even to those who in their ignorance speak unkind. For, remember, how they buffeted thy Lord! Let thy watchword be: "Through the power of the Christ in me, I can—and *will*—do that He would have me do! Trusting only in Him I will press on—*on*—to the mark of the calling whereunto He has called, and does call me."   281-22

5 / Patient Waiting

 A belief in life includes an acceptance of life's cyclic nature. To persist when passivity is called for exhibits a lack of faith. Here is a time to wait, not impatiently, not anxious to continue on one's way, but with the joyful knowledge that this is the way. This inner certainty is true courage, which will eventually transcend any obstacle.

(Q) Please give any advice which will be helpful to me at this time.

(A) Learn again patience, yet persistent patience, active patience—not merely passive. Patience does not mean merely waiting, but as it does for those that would induce nature to comply with nature's laws. So with patience, comply with patience's laws, working together with love, purpose, faith, hope, charity; giving expression to these in thy daily associations with those ye meet; making thy daily problems as real as real life-experiences, purposeful in every way.

And let not thy heart be troubled; ye believe in God. Believe in His promises, too, that as ye sow, so in the fullness of time and in material experience these things shall come about.   1968-5

For, as given, "In patience possess ye your souls." This does not mean sitting down and waiting, but with prayer, with fortitude, with patience, with persistence, meet each day with that necessary fullness of purpose as to be ready to be used as He would see fit. And, as has been given, as each approaches in such a way and manner He opens the way for that necessary for the meeting of every need, materially, mentally, spiritually, in thine experience.   333-3

(Q) About how long will it take before she will be able to walk?

(A) This to be sure depends upon the responses of the body. Whether long or short (but this should be within one cycle), the results will be worthy of the patience, the care. 1328-1

As has been indicated, and as has been outlined, this will require the cycle of change in the body. To lose faith, or patience, or confidence, is to allow the child in its development—and the man—to be handicapped in this experience. Either do it, or allow it to go undone!3873-2

Even though an entity in the earth's plane, in this life, may reach the years of fourscore and ten, these are as but moments in eternity. How oft would it be the better that each soul weigh those things in its experience that it knows! and to consider that someone cares; for He, the Lord of light, the way, the truth, the bright and morning star, the lily of the valley, the rose of Sharon, awaits—as has given His angels charge concerning thee, that thou walkest in the light. Be patient; for in patience, in waiting on the Lord, in being kind and gentle, do ye become aware of His presence in the earth. Not unto vainglorying, but be ye joyous in the service that would make of thee—in thy temptations, in thy trials—as one that would be a bright and morning star, a hope to thy fellow man, a prop to those that falter and stumble, a refuge to those that are troubled in body and mind! 640-1

6 / Evaluating Strife

 Because the way is long and confusing at times, one may easily set off in a wrong direction with the sincerest of intentions. Certainly, it is well to take care in preparation for the journey. But if it becomes apparent that the way chosen is beset with conflict, it is well to pause and consider the motivations that brought one to this uneasy place. To insist on continuing, when continuation is questionable, is to invite disaster. Until the conflict is resolved, do not pursue any other enterprise.

But if ye are attempting to have thy physical body doing just as it pleases, thy mental body controlled by "What will other people say?" and thy spiritual body and mind shelved only for good occasions and for the good impressions that you may make occasionally, there *cannot* be other than confusion!

These as given are not merely sayings; they answer to that which has been and is thy turmoil in the present. Look *within!*

For if there is trouble in thy mind, in thy body, in thy spirit—or purpose, or mind; sin lieth at that door.

1537-1

In the present there is the love of things that are easy, which arises from the harkenings of the inmost self; the love of those things that are true arises from that period also—and hence the two are often in conflict within self. O that all would know that the greater conflict ever to each soul is between its own self's experiences as compared to that it *has* experienced!   541-1

There are the tendencies, then, towards mysticism and the psychic. These conflict also one with another.

The tendencies towards the Oriental truths often conflict with Occidental habits of individuals, causing in the entity's activities those periods of confusions to the entity itself. 3411-1

(Q) [137]: I have certain thoughts regarding the Association's environments and condition. Can you give me counsel of those?

(A) In the interior forces of self, there is seen that no higher counsel may be had than that as may be gained by self through that attunement of self to that power. Heed none other. Let no conflict of any nature separate thine self from that ability to attune self with Him, and in counsel of every character He will guide, whether it be of those that pertain to material, mental or spiritual. He was in the flesh thine brother. 140-35

(Q) Is it best for me to assume an impersonal attitude toward all material conditions around me (as it was told me in regard to the Cayce Hospital), or should I take definite stands?

(A) In the light of that just given, judge ye. For when definite stands of a material way conflict with definite stands of other individuals in *their* material way, conflicts ensue. But let thy desires, thy purposes, thy aims, be as one with that which is shown thee through the meditations from within. 288-37

7 / Leadership

When crisis threatens, what is called for is self-organization, inner strength and constancy in what is right. To proceed without regard for high ideals is always wrong. One is increased by one's generous behavior toward others. Inspire them so that you will receive their support. Provide others with the strength to act. That is true leadership.

The abilities to be the leader in the community is not too much for the entity to think or feel, or for it to act either! It doesn't have to brag or boast about it, for then the effectiveness is lost and it becomes self-purpose; but in the activities of Mars, Jupiter, Saturn, Mercury, we may find the helpful influences of a universal consciousness applied in the diplomatic manner that is a part of the experience will bring good in the experience and in the environs of the entity. And these will be sound judgments and be unfoldments and developments for the entity that will be sowing the seeds of that the entity sets as its ideal.   3590-1

As indicated in the seal, the entity may play upon the emotions of others or it may use them for stepping-stones or stumbling blocks. It may use opportunities to raise others to the point of anxiety or to the point where they would spend their souls for the entity; using them either as buildings or as serpents or scorpions in its emotions. It may love very deeply, either for the universal consciousness or for gratifying only of self or the physical emotions.   3637-1

(Q) How can I better prepare myself for the work I have chosen and for leadership?

(A) By prayer and meditation. It *is* innate and natural, yet the basis of service must be as of the ideal; not merely idealistic—for that indicates unattainable, but "Be ye *perfect,* even as I am perfect," said He. This then is in purpose, in intent, in hope, in application. This is the manner to attain to leadership.

Ask no one to do that ye would not do thyself. Ask no one to do that the *Lord* thy Master did not do.   2746-1

(Q) Who can give body the best leadership or counsel for his spiritual development?

(A) That which may be found in St. John.   282-4

And the abilities are here to accomplish whatever the entity would choose to set its mind to, so long as the entity trusts not in the might of self, but in His grace, His power, His might. Be mindful ever of that, in thy understanding in thy own wisdom, much may be accomplished; but be rather thou the channel through which He, God, the Father, may manifest His power—in whatever may be the chosen activity of the entity.   3183-1

8 / Grouping

Often the best way to meet danger is by joining with others. Let yourself go to experience being in close sympathy with those around you. Pursue common goals and pleasures, and it will give you a better perspective on yourself. Discover the groups to which you naturally belong. The sharing of responsibilities fosters one humanity.

First, as has been oft given, there is *strength* in unity of purpose—for, as has been given, "Where two or three gather together in my name, I am in the midst of same," and if in that name ye ask *believing* ye shall receive according to the faith that lies within each and every one of you; for God is not mocked, and whatsoever ye sow, so shall ye reap. As ye build, so shall the *structure* be. If such a structure becomes top-heavy, or there is presented those things that make for strife, contention, selfishness, these beget the children thereof. If same is founded in love, in peace, these beget the children thereof.   254-52

(Q) Am I devoting too much of my time to committee or community work?
(A) Not devoting too much, provided that advantage is taken *of* those associations as brought about in committee work, in community work; taking advantage of that insight as is given into the affairs of others, and use same—Don't abuse! but use same!   322-1

While it may appear that some of the things that might have been accomplished materially have passed the entity by, these abilities in the present should be used in a constructive, creative manner, and thus be ever a contributor to the welfare of whatever community the entity may be a part of, or group; making those with whom the entity may associate a little better, thinking and feeling a little bit improved by the knowledge, the abilities, the activities that may be accomplished in the young from the abilities latent within the entity.   3424-1

Every phase of human experience and human relationship must be taken into consideration; just as indicated from that given, that we *are* our brother's keeper.

Then if those in position to give of their means, their wealth, their education, their position, *do not* take these things into consideration, there must be that leveling that will come.   3976-19

For there is set before thee those choices to be made, as to *whom* ye will serve.

As to *manners*, then, in which each soul shall conduct self as respecting this as an individual organization, it has oft been given that this is not under any schism or ism or any individual tenet other than that which has been of old, "I *am* my brother's keeper!" That should be the cry that should be in the heart of every member, every individual, *"I am my brother's keeper!"*

Then so live, so act, so conduct thyself in thy dealings with thy fellow man day by day that they who are astray may be set aright.   254-91

9 / Humble Strength

Here is not a time for action, except on a limited basis. One may possess the strength, but the conditions are not favorable. Be moderate. The cycle of preparation is not yet complete. The inner person should be strong, but the outer person should manifest gentleness. Any progress must be subtly achieved.

(Q) Kindly give me any advice that will benefit me spiritually, physically, mentally.

(A) . . . Study to show self approved unto thy Maker, thy better self. Purposefulness, then, in that done or accomplished or thought, that brings *constructive* influence and experience into the hearts and minds and lives of individuals.

It isn't the great things. No great deeds of valor are accomplished without *ages* of preparation in the *soul* of one that accomplishes same.

It is just being kind, just being gentle, just being patient, *first* with self and self's relationships to thy fellow man.

These are not principles that are for the church alone, nor for the lodge, nor social organizations; but more and more the principles to be applied in the experience of the business man, the social man, in the everyday life. Thus may better the glory of the Lord shine through thine experience.

How much greater in the experience of each soul to at the end of any given day have the satisfaction of the best within self say to thee, "Well done!" than to have all the *glory* of man that you have tricked or have overstepped in some manner that may have been for material gain!

416-7

And in the application, study self. Be humble, but not timid; be positive, but not in that determination of rule or ruin. But rather in that as was given—mercy, justice, patience, love, long-suffering, brotherly kindness, and forgetting those things that easily beset one in grudges or hatreds or hard feelings—but rather study others.

1402-1

Open the door for those that cry aloud for a knowledge that God is within the reach of those that will put their hand to *doing;* just being kind—not a great deed as men count greatness, but just being gentle and patient and loving even with those that would despitefully use thee. For the beauties of the Lord are with those that seek to know and *witness* for Him among men.

That is thy mission, that is thy purpose, in this material experience. 1436-1

(Q) How can I still further advance into the perfection I seek to attain in the Father's eyes and the fellow man's?

(A) Put into practice day by day that as *is* known. Not some great deed or act, or speech, but line upon line, precept upon precept, here a little, there a little. Not as sounding of trumpets as to what is being accomplished, but in the quiet of thine own conscience lay the plans for that that may be accomplished, and in the acts day by day so build that as conforms to *His* way; for, as He has given, those that seek to know the Lord and do His biddings shall not go empty-handed; neither shall his seed beg bread. 257-78

10 / Treading Wisely

 Step forward with care toward your goal. If one proceeds respectfully when one is near danger, behaving decorously, achievement is possible. Here is a time for discriminating between things, classifying most and least importants. But in so doing, be careful not to seem prejudicial. Those around you will respond to your well-ordered, step-by-step progress with your life.

These, then, are the conditions as are to be met, that there may be brought discernment in the mental, that it, the mental, may build in the physical conditions that to which the body, through same, may attain. O that men and women would learn to discern the manifestations of the Lord, as He in His goodness gives to men that which will—would they but bring it to the gift of man— bring the discerning of the light, the life, and the love as may be manifested among the Sons of men! 2241-1

In the application of self, this entity has gained the ability of discernment, and in the way of using the *little* in *hand* to gain the greater *understanding* of the whole.
115-1

Keep the faith. Walk in the light. Let no darkness be in thee at all. For *He is* the light, the truth and the way, and He is willing—if thou wilt but walk with Him. 792-1

(Q) Please advise [257] as you did years ago in the Albert Pick-Federal matter, what he should do step by step to again be successful in this field.
(A) As given and outlined here, and given again: First take all those situations that confront the body from ev-

ery angle, and after analyzing them, comparing self and self's abilities, self's qualifications, the qualifications, the tactics and the policies of those with whom the body would associate, and who would be the better. Then work and *pay* that necessary in effort, time, endeavor, to make the connections in such a manner as to meet every situation.   257-138

In the application does the knowledge come of what *is* to be accomplished by self, in the step by step, line by line, that others may know of that promise that *is* to each individual that may be one with Him. Be not unmindful that those met in the way are seekers also, and are the Israel of the Lord.   262-30

(Q) How should we present it to one who has lost faith in Creative Force?
(A) . . . Be not overcome with those things that make for discouragements, for *He* will supply the strength. Lean upon the arm of the *Divine* within thee, giving not place to thoughts of vengeance or discouragements. Give not vent to those things that create prejudice. And, most of all, be *unselfish!* For selfishness is sin, before first thine self, then thine neighbor and thy God.
Love ye one another. Give as ye have received. 254-87

11 / Peace

Live in peace with powerful forces and influences around you. Strengthen yourself to be able to meet inevitable hardship but still maintain a peaceful centeredness. Cultivate a kind of internal order which allows you to concentrate peacefully and completely on what is at hand in the present moment.

(Q) How can I overcome the feeling of frustration?

(A) Know in what you have believed and who is the author. Then live by it, and live with it and you will find peace. For, the promise is, as from Him, "It must indeed be that offenses come, but woe unto him by whom they come."

Be not disturbed, as He gives, because of frustrations. Know, "I have overcome the world, and if you abide in me, I bring peace." And peace is far from frustration.

2528-3

And all may be on fire with the powers that may manifest through them; becoming less and less self-centered, less and less selfish; and more and more at peace and in harmony with those experiences that are theirs in the going about to show forth His love, through the application of that each are gaining through their walks with Him in prayer, in meditation. 262-38

Each has been chosen as a channel, and each in its own way—and not alone of self, but manifesting life through love will bring the Spirit's reaction in the daily experiences of every soul. For, they are one—*all* believe, all have heard. Then, let them that have eyes see, and ears hear, what the Spirit saith unto them in such meditation in the *inner* self.

For, from the abundance of the heart the mouth speaketh; and the love of the Father through the Son constraineth all, if each will be less selfish, less self-centered, more desirous of showing forth *His* love, His abundant mercy, His peace, His harmony, that comes from being quiet in the Lord, being joyous in service, being happy in whatsoever state ye find self; knowing that he whom the Lord loveth him doth He call into service, if each soul will but seek to know *His* way rather than "my way or thy way." Let thy yeas be yea in the Lord. Let thine understanding take hold on the things of the spirit, for they are alone eternal.   262-46

For, whatever the entity chooses to do may be accomplished; provided that the ego does not get ahead of the I AM in the entity's experience. For, if self is placed first and foremost, this is as the "little book" which when eaten turns to gall within the experience of the entity. Using the abilities in any direction to the glory of the Creative Forces may bring honor and fame, as well as much of this world's goods. Allowing self to become self-centered, the best friends may be as outcasts from the entity, and peace and harmony within self be as naught.
                                        3126-1

Yet thou, in thine own self, hast that which may set the *world* on fire for the Lord; that of sincerity with self. Keep thine heart pure. Thou mayest bring peace and harmony to many by the gentleness of the Christ words through thine own self.   281-19

12 / Frustrating Obstruction

The cooperative conjunction of the spiritual and physical has passed, and the balance of conditions tips toward the unfavorable. You are caught between the desire to move and a stagnant environment. If one has developed an inner focus through which to maintain the positive perspective, one slides through the difficulties. One should quietly maintain one's self-esteem, avoiding temptation and the negative influences that press in.

(Q) Why are all my undertakings mostly confronted with such difficulty?

(A) Through difficulty has the entity gained much of the experiences in the past, as *well* as in the present. Those that *overcome* difficulties may wear the crown. Those that succumb *to* difficulties are counting themselves unworthy. Keep the faith as *is* being builded *through* the love influence, putting behind thee those things that so easily beset, looking forward to the mark of the high calling as is set in Him—through the *ideals* as have been set. 2141-1

Be not unmindful that there is that way which brings self the awareness of His presence, God's presence, the Master's presence, and the better self that has experienced—through the eons of time—those relationships to the mental things that have presented themselves as problems, conditions, experiences; but He has promised, "I will stand in thy stead" in such conditions, if ye will but put your trust, your faith, in Him; for He *is* the way. 274-3

While there might be much given as to that which has caused or produced the conditions, these should be rather viewed by the entity, the body [716], in this attitude: "The physical conditions that have come upon me are those most necessary for my own soul's development." While there have been periods of antagonism and of belittling self, making for the berating of the circumstance, the conditions that have come upon self, know that these conditions have given thee the opportunity to see that in it all there has been given the privilege for others to express in their activity the true spirit of love, that creative influence that is worshiped by man as God.

716-2

(Q) How can body avoid constant restlessness and sense of frustration and uselessness? Why doesn't her home life and her charities satisfy her?

(A) These will, when they are made one with the mental, physical and spiritual well-being; for these have been kept *separated*—and one as not knowing what the other did, but in the coordinating of the physical and mental and spiritual well-being, of that as may be accomplished in the home, in the charity, or in the associations socially, these should be *ever* with the eye single of that, "whatsoever my hands find to do, that will I do, with an eye single of showing, manifesting, living, *being*, my concept of the Divine."

454-1

(Q) Why do I suffer acutely at times from a sense of frustration?

(A) This is partly physical, partly the karmic and the *form* of the ideas in relationship to the real ideals of the entity.

2329-1

13 / Trusting Fellowship

When circumstances require, as they do here, that many unite to achieve a goal, what is needed is that their separate drives be discarded in favor of an organized, collective effort. Joining together in trust for mutual good builds a social structure with balance and support. The quality of open sincerity helps to remove the walls of distrust that often divide people. Clarity of purpose and commitment to common values build sustaining fellowship.

(Q) Please help me understand why it is so difficult for me to obtain cooperation and sincere help of individuals in presenting Furfluf.

(A) Oft the very misunderstanding is brought about by distrust of self, distrust of others, and the wonderment of the activities about self.

So, just be that which is known to be—not self-righteous, but righteous in other respects; that is, to others in gentleness, patience, kindness, long-suffering—these create the atmosphere of trust.

Ye will not be trusted if ye do not trust others. 1000-19

If the entity will apply in self that it *knows* to do—not as something that applies to self alone, but that applies to self in its relationships to others—the results will be apparent. Ye *apply* thy love, if ye would have others love thee! Ye do trust others and ye *are* the trust and the hope, if ye would have hope or expect others to have hope and trust in thee!   3078-1

(Q) [69]: What is the extreme test of fellowship?
(A) Doing unto others as ye would have them do unto

you is the extreme test of fellowship. Without same ye may not wholly please God. 262-22

(Q) [307]: Can brotherhood exist among men without true fellowship?
(A) Fellowship is first brotherhood, a pattern of—or a shadow of—what fellowship is; for, as has been given, all one sees manifest in a material world is but a reflection or a shadow of the real or the spiritual life. Brotherhood, then, is an expression of the fellowship that exists in the *spiritual* life. 262-23

. . . the trust must be in *Him,* not *in* the group! The group is only lending their power, their ability, to make more aware the needs of each individual so seeking of that power! for He hath knowledge of that we have need of before we ask, but "Ask and ye shall receive." 281-9

The entity gained throughout that period; for, from its early experience, as will be seen, there has been the consciousness of the needs for man in the low estate as well as in the high estate to be dependent one upon the other; yet the needs for the trust, the confidence to be established upon a principle or a basis for the betterment of each group. This was the basis upon which the entity applied itself in that period. 2902-1

14 / Harvesting Wealth

 Wealth without greed; possession without desire. Power used in the name of good reaps great benefit for the user, bringing him into a balance with the cosmic supplier, and giving him a truer perspective as to the nature and origin of wealth. True wealth is greater than money, and the harvest that nourishes the spirit comes from finding one's role and responsibilies in a greater order.

But all power, all force, arises from one source; and those that have same are only lended same by an All-Wise and Merciful Creator as talents to be used in His vineyard.

For each entity, each soul, *is* his brother's keeper!

189-3

In understanding, does strength, power and might come.

Take this and keep it with thee in thy heart, and in thine mind always. With power of money, with position, and wealth, comes greater responsibility. But ye know in whom ye believed, and He is able to keep you against that day.

137-125

Man's answer to everything has been *power*—power of money, power of position, power of wealth, power of this, that or the other. This has *never* been *God's* way, will never be God's way. Rather little by little, line upon line, here a little, there a little, each thinking rather of the other fellow, as that that has kept the world in the various ways of being intact—where there were ten, even, many a city, many a nation, has been kept from destruction.

3976-8

(Q) What would be the most harmonious and remunerative business for me?

(A) ... a strong, healthy, well-balanced physical body may find, with its activities to make for same, a budgeting of its efforts in mental and physical and spiritual things ... for with health may come wealth if it is needed in that for the spiritual development.

Would that most people would gain that knowledge that if they are attempting to live a normal life, if wealth is necessary for their soul development it is a portion of their experience!   498-1

(Q) How may the material activities and the spiritual purpose be coordinated?

(A) That in the material world is a shadow of that in the celestial or spiritual world. Then, the material manifestations of spiritual impulse or activity must be in keeping or in attune with that which has its inception in *spiritual* things. For, the *mind* of man *is* the builder; and if the beginning is in spiritual life, and the mental body sees, acts upon, is motivated only by the spiritual, then the physical result will be in keeping with that thou hast sown ...

If the activities make for the exaltation of the mind, the body, or the position, power, wealth or fame, *these* are of the earth earthy.

Not that there should not be the material things, but the result of spiritual activity—*not* the result of the desires for that which the material things bring *as* power to a soul.   524-2

15 / Modesty

Whatever the conditions, one must take great care to maintain a modest equilibrium in one's thoughts and activities. An overbalance—giving too great or too little an emphasis to an aspect of experience—will impede one's progress toward the goal. Becoming too all-consumed by your ideas and projects is a form of self-consciousness to be carefully avoided.

(Q) Is there any way in which the entity at this time could serve her Father-God, as she has an intense desire to do so?

(A) As indicated—it is not by might, nor by some great deed (as the entity saw illustrated in that experience), nor by something that may be spoken of by others, but as He has given so oft, it is here a little, there a little, line upon line, precept upon precept; *sowing* the fruits of the spirit, *leaving* the fruition of same to God!

So oft do individuals stumble over their own abilities, because of not seeing, not experiencing, great revolutions because of their attempts.

Remember, as it was told to those of old, as it was told to *thee* by those who answered when ye beheld Him enter the glory of the clouds, the sky—"Think not He has left thee, for His promise has been, Lo, I am with thee always, even unto the end of the world."   1877-2

(Q) How could I eliminate self-consciousness and fear when addressing an audience?

(A) That's just what we have been talking about, in entering into the silence, by not as rote, but as entering into the consciousness of that of the Creative Forces as gives to all that as was promised, "Take no thought of what ye shall say, for in the self-same hour will it be given thee." When one has reached, and does reach, that consciousness of the Divine's activity within self, then *self's* consciousness, or self-consciousness, is laid aside.

666-1

(Q) Do you recommend that during the treatments suggested *any* of the following exercises be taken?

(A) [Interrupting] As indicated here, there is not the great amount of exercise to be taken. Not that the body is just to sit down and rest and do nothing, but no specific exercises until the compound has been taken; then *all* forms of exercising, whether swimming, walking, rowing, golfing, or that, would be well for the body—in moderation—but control the exercises, rather than the exercises controlling the body.

498-1

. . . for with all things let them be done in moderation, in decency and in order, and in a way keeping to these truths as set in the way as has been set for the law as is known to the entity concerning that necessary in self to bring the best normal gift to the world of the position occupied by entity. Then do it.

136-20

Better to be moderate in all things, whether eating or drinking, or smoking, or what! *Moderation* is the key to success or longevity!

294-130

16 / Enthusiastic Rededication

There is the danger of carelessness due to weariness. Enthusiastic passion for the journey must be rekindled. It behooves one to pause and reestablish oneself spiritually, even dedicating oneself to the will of the cosmic. In this way one can lessen the possibility of directional error and also create the personal aura necessary in attracting cooperation from others. Rally your forces and set them moving.

For, as those laws that become as but watchwords to many on the tower, there is a whole day's work before thee each day, with all its glorious opportunities of seeing the glory of the Lord manifested by thine own acts!

Yet if that which confronts thee makes for discouragement, harshness of words, lack of enthusiasm, or those things that make for doubts or fears, the opportunity has turned its back—and what *is* the outlook? Doubt and fear!

Study, then, to show thyself approved, *each day! Do what* thou *knowest* to do, to be aright! Then *leave it alone!* God giveth the increase! Thy worry, thy anxiety, only will produce disorder in thine *own* mind!

For the application in self, the *try,* the effort, the energy expended in the proper direction, is all that is required of *thee.* God giveth the increase.   601-11

To be named as a vice-president doesn't make the body any more *capable,* or his abilities any greater; neither does it increase the valuation in the eyes of the public—other than the ability to *serve* the public in that capacity in a greater degree. Raised to a position in a public service only gives the individual the opportunity to serve the public in a more noble manner. Position by name means little! Position by the *acquiring* of the abilities to *fill* the position means much! Fill self with enthusiasm for *service*, rather than glory for that *attained*.

257-32

(Q) Do adverse astrological influences have anything to do with his apparent inability to gain strength and enthusiasm again?

(A) Not anything to do! These must be *met* and *not followed!* It is like this: You don't feel like moving about, but move a little bit anyway—and this gains strength!

556-12

(Q) What can I do to regain the pep and enthusiasm which I need to be successful with [257] in the . . . Furniture line in N.Y.?

(A) First have the physical conditions corrected, and get out of the attitude of trying to hedge or stall or trying to make for the easy way or the shortcuts.   1414-1

. . . if the efforts and activities—as we find—are expended in the right direction, this characteristic, this ability to express the personality, the enthusiasm that the entity is able to work itself up to on any proposition—either mental, spiritual or material (if convinced of the sincerity, the plausibility and possibilities), may be expanded upon by the entity in such a manner as to produce enthusiasm in the efforts of those with whom the entity may surround self in any endeavor.   342-2

17 / Seeking

The search for truth is fraught with obstacles and disappointments. Sincere seeking means making many choices along the way, and selecting one way at a crossroads means foreclosing another way. Even though mistakes and errors sometimes arise—even though gains along the way are offset by losses—keep true to your search and the ideal that inspires it.

(Q) What is the *right road* for me to take which I have not yet found?

(A) As indicated, first know *what is thy ideal!* There is none other. Let it be in the spiritual forces, *not* in the material. Seek to know *the Christ Consciousness!*

(Q) Why are there opposing forces in me that cause conflict and confusion?

(A) As has been seen through the experiences in the earth; yet *will* to do that thou knowest *today,* and then it will be given thee what to do tomorrow.   1167-2

Seek first, then, within self as to what is thy ideal. Hold fast, thou, to that strength as thou perceived that prompted the hearts and minds and bodies of those that served their fellow man without seeking for self-glorification. And with thy ideal set in the spiritual things, ye may find and ye will know the truth that was in Him. For the truth shall indeed make you free, when ye come to the understanding of same as ye apply it in thy relations to thy fellow man.   877-1

For an idea and an ideal are two different things—an ideal is that that may be sought for, while an idea may lead into troubled waters.   5502-2

Self-development, as the individual then makes for the personality in the material life and in the spiritual life, makes the associations with the creative influences in every walk, in every act, in every deed. And be ye joyous in this service.

How may such be accomplished in the present? Know in what thou has believed, knowing that He is able to keep thee against any experience that may bring fear or doubt. For, by faith are ye healed and that not of yourself, but is the gift of the Father to those that seek and those who have made Him that He has given in the earth *as* the ideal.   439-2

(Q) What counsel have you for Mrs. [Eileen] Garrett's spiritual development?

(A) Present self in thine own inner conscience in such a way and manner that answers for the conscience within self of its own soul development. And as the soul remains true to that which is its ideal from within, it may never give that other than constructive in its speech with those that seek to know the mysteries of soul and self-development; that has made of itself a channel through which men may approach those mysteries of life, and their activities in the minds, the hearts and the souls of men.   507-1

18 / Work

One's work is the focal point between the old and the new; between one's past and the future; between parent and offspring. Experience the conflict between the expectations of your parents or tradition, on the one hand—your own needs and calling, on the other. Let work be your application of high personal standards and in so doing resolve the conflict between old and new.

Then what would ye do with thy abilities? As ye give to others, not hating them, to know more of the Universal Forces, so may ye have the more, for, God is love.

Do that, and ye will bring bettered conditions for yourself. Work where you are. As was given to those who were called, "The ground upon which ye stand is holy."

Begin where you are. If there are the needs for other environs, these will be shown—will be given thee.

4021-1

What then is the purpose of the entity's activity in the consciousness of mind? That it, the entity, may *know* itself to *be* itself and part of the Whole; not the Whole but one *with* the Whole; and thus retaining its individuality, knowing itself to be itself yet one with the purposes of the First Cause that called it, the entity, into *being*, into the awareness, into the consciousness of itself.

That is the purpose, that is the cause of *being*. 826-11

(Q) What is my mission in this incarnation?

(A) As has been indicated, again dissemination of truth in its relationship to things, to conditions, to individuals, to nations.

(Q) Am I making progress in that direction?

(A) You are at the crossroad—the choice is to be made! Choose the spiritual import!

(Q) Should I proceed with the work I am planning for greater harmony in the industry; between management and labor?

(A) Provided the spirituality is included. For the spirit giveth life; the law killeth; the spirit giveth life!

(Q) Will this work prove as beneficial as I think it will?

(A) Do it for the cause of Him, who is truth and ye may leave the results to Him and it will not be a failure.

5395-1

Ever, *ever*, the fruits of the Spirit in their awareness; long-suffering, brotherly love, patience, kindness, gentleness, *hope* and faith!

If ye in thy activities in any manner with thy fellow man destroy these in the minds, in the heart of thy fellow man, ye are not only slipping but ye have taken hold on the path of destruction.

Then so love, so act, so *think* that others *seeing* thy good works, thy hopes that ye bring, thy faith that ye manifest, thy patience that ye show, may *also* glorify Him.

For that cause, for that purpose ye entered into the materiality in the present. 826-11

19 / Persuasive Authority

Act with alertness to your influence and power over others. Be persuasive through honesty and sincerity. The use of force is discouraged. The best kind of persuasion is by being an example through your own words and deeds.

As given, it is well that the exercises that are required be required to be carried out in toto; not ever other than in the most loving way and manner; not by being driven or forced, but by the persuasive activities; for there is that language in every clime that bespeaks of that activity in our material plane—*love*.

In *this* manner may the greater strength, the greater developments come for the body . . .

While the body should not be *pampered*, there should be more and more the persuasive and loving-kindness method used; for remember, as it has been given, those who would minister to the awakening of the powers and forces that are manifest in *this* body will not lose their reward.   758-36

In Venus we find the home and the beauties of friendships; with Uranus as well as Mercury bringing about influences of wisdom, strength, and unseen influence among groups of masses through which the entity may—and does—influence others.

This almost becomes then an unconscious influence that the entity bears.   910-4

(Q) What should the next step be for those in this office in regard to the establishment of the New York group?

(A) Be rather insistent, in a gentle and persuasive

manner, to each that might be a portion of the group to induce that this be accomplished in as speedy manner as possible; giving to each again and again the necessities for that they would foster, they would cherish in their experience for that they received, and are receiving, and may receive through such a channel! If this is not *worthy*, then—forget it!   254-64

(Q) How may those desiring to assist this body best obtain the cooperation of the body in following this treatment?
(A) This, as has been given, will require some persistence, some persuasive powers, in gentleness and in kindness, and with the *reasoning* of the body as respecting same. We will find that the body will have a tendency to adhere to these, then to leave them off—but be persistent in following these as given.   5683-1

. . . hold fast to those judgments that are of the Creative Forces. Know that only in Him is there truth and light *and* authority. For *all* power is of *His* giving, and is lent to the sons of men as *opportunities* for expressions of the Creative Forces.   956-1

20 / Right View

 To truly know a thing one must experience it and contemplate inwardly its meaning. To understand other people one must come into contact with their lives and see their deepest needs. Learn this way to be sympathetic to their point of view. Then one can teach with true sympathy and what one has to give is well received. All depends on gaining the right view of life.

Hold fast to that ideal. And in thy dealings with thy brother, meet rather that as would be if conditions were reversed; being patient, being understanding; not as preachments but rather as following of precepts and living the ideal that is manifest in the word of the entity.

And let thy prayer ever be, in this direction:

Father, God! Speak Thou to me in word that I may understand. But let me, O God, speak ever to my brother in deeds, rather than words.   2524-4

That the soul—a portion, an expression of God's desire for companionship—might find expression, the souls of men and women came into being; that there might be that which would make each soul, then, as a fit companion for that realm. There is the necessity of fitting itself through the experiences of all phases and realms of existence, then; that it, the soul, may not cause disruption in the realm of beauty, harmony, strength of divinity in its companionships with that Creative Force.

Hence the experiences, if we will gain that deeper comprehension of same, are but opportunities; for in whatsoever state of consciousness one *finds* self, the awakening is from the desire of the Father that each soul shall continue to have *its* thread of gold that runs through each conscious force for its companionship with Him.

So the use or application of that in hand makes for the awareness within self of *its,* the soul's, relationships to the Creative Force.   805-4

For ye live, ye move in an environ of dimensions according to the awareness and application of thyself to these influences in thy activity. It is not then what ye think or what ye say that counts, but what thy soul desires, what thy soul hopes for, what thy soul manifests in thy relationships to these environs; that are opportunities for the application of that understanding ye *may* have at any given period of manifestation.   2608-1

... as you each become conscious in your own experience of the movement *of* the influences *through* the body upon the various stages of awareness, there comes a determination, a desire, a longing for the greater light. To him, to her that is faithful, there shall be given a *crown* of light. And His name shall be above every name; for ye that have seen the light know in whom thou hast believed, and know that in thine own body, thine own mind, there is set the temple of the living God, and that it may function in thy dealings with thy fellow man in such measures that ye become as rivers of light, as fountains of knowledge, as mountains of strength, as the pastures for the hungry, as the rest for the weary, as the strength for the weak. Keep the faith.   281-28

21 / Removing Restraints

The bridle that has constrained you grows tighter and tighter. Bite through it while there is still a chance to be free of unjust restraint. Stand up for yourself. Act not out of a spirit of revenge or anger, but simply to assert your true self and its needs.

(Q) Should the body be guided by suggestions made by relatives and friends? or follow his own ideas in spite of everything?

(A) If that towards ideas are in keeping with the *ideals,* follow those. Have *ideals,* not *ideas!* Ideas may be as thoughts, made criminal or miracles. Be sure the *ideal* is proper. Follow that irrespective of outside influence. Know self is right, and then go straight ahead. So live each and every day that you may look any man in the face and tell him to go to hell!   1739-6

. . . there is produced by same humbleness—not as has been in some instances in the entity's self—not the lording of others. For as He gave, who was, who is, who ever will be the manifestation of the Spirit—which is true psychic force—he that will be the greatest will be the servant of all. Not necessarily being as a doormat, but ever willing, ever helpful—but to the glory of God, to the honor of self. Not to the glory of self in any manner or way, but in humbleness preferring one another. 3548-1

(Q) At this time, is there anything else that you would care to say to me about the past, present or future?

(A) So live and so act with self as to be able to look every man or individual in the face and tell him to "Go to hell"; or so act, in that way and manner that there is known within self that there is that activity which *can-not* be questioned, either by the superior or by the office boy, or by the drayman. So act, in that way and activity of forces, that that as is done becomes a *living* example of that that the body would present to its Creator; *not* being *ashamed* of that which it acts upon, *through* or how, but in a way acceptable to self, to God—to thy Creator!

270-28

(Q) Is there any advice for greater development of character?

(A) Study to know thyself in relationship to that ye choose as thy ideal. And let that ideal be set in Him, who is the way, the truth and the light.

This does not mean becoming goody-goody, no—far from it! Be able to look *everyman* in the face and tell him to go to hell—but *live* as He did, the lovely Nazarene!

2869-1

The entity because of his indecisions at times allows others to take advantage of him. The entity must learn to be self-assertive; not egotistical but self-assertive—from a knowledge of the relationship of self with the material world.

3018-1

22 / Beauty

One comes to a time in life when beauty and tasteful adornment reflect the workings of the transcendent, universal spirit. Like a wedding where the bride and groom call forth inner and outer beauty, you have come to a time in life when that which is beautiful lifts your spirits.

God is not mocked, and man—nor woman—can fool themselves into making themselves believe that there is *not* that which repays many, many times for that effort in *whatever* thing given out; for that given out will return to the one spending self. If we would have life, give it. If we would have love, make ourselves lovely. If we would have beauty within our lives, make our lives beautiful. If we would have beauty in body or mind, or soul, create that atmosphere and that which brings about life itself will bring those forces; for the *spirit* is willing, the flesh is contrary—as well as weak. In the *spirit* is strength. Give that strength as an opportunity of manifesting itself in thine life! as it is manifested in the lives of those whom the entity contacts, for the kind word turneth away wrath, even as the haughty look or the unkind word stirreth up and maketh for troubles in the lives of many. Make thine life *beautiful,* and it becomes more worthwhile. 2096-1

Cultivate those abilities for making the beautiful tales of those influences or things that apparently are the commonplace. For it is the commonplace that wields the greater influence in the lives of individuals in any home, in *any* community. These may be added to in such ways and manners as to later, in thy experience, become channels through which great blessings may come to others. 2037-1

For, we live only the one moment at the time. Those that are transient will pass away—and only the earthly pass; but that love that can sustain, that love that does sustain in all the hours of trial, all the hours of temptations, all the hours of sufferings, abides with thee still. Keep—*keep*—the heart singing. Look deeper into the heart of the rose. *Listen* to the song of the bird. See the paintings of His face in the setting and the rising sun. See the loveliness in the moonbeam that turns all into the radiance of His glory.   410-2

So in thy dealings with others, with thy problems with others, in thy daily associations, in thy home, in thy activities—remember to evaluate *every* phase of an experience and to stress the beautiful, minimize the faults. For, this is sowing the seed of beauty in the spirit of truth; and that, too, will blossom in thy life and in thy dealings with others.   2448-2

(Q) Please explain why I seem to sob from within.
(A) As indicated, frustration of ideals brought about by apparent circumstance, in which much of that beautiful has been subjugated in the experience of the entity.
                          2339-1

23 / Staying Put

During a period of adversity, don't push forward. Striking out or acting out will not accomplish anything. Although one must arrest his forward progress, it is possible at least to maintain the position already attained. By the generous giving to those who are less fortunate, one fulfills the responsibility of position and thereby does not lose ground.

In whatsoever state one finds (as he has found himself) oneself, make self content; not satisfied, but content, ever working toward that oneness of mind (of body, of will, with the development), or universal, or psychic forces. Do not war against these conditions. Make of conditions the stepping-stones to the development necessary to meet the daily needs in physical, in mental, in financial. 137-7

Like begets like. *This* is infallible.

If there is the desire, then, to *force* an issue, there will be just as strong opposition the other way; and even when an issue is forced, has anything been gained? For the moment, perhaps—but this association should be, if properly founded and based (as it has been in the past, in most of its activities), of a longer duration than one generation. 270-31

(Q) [Explain] "Content but not satisfied."

(A) Content in that "Have Thy way, Lord. Use me as a channel. Not my will but Thine be done!" That is content.

Satisfied means gratified, and is the beginning of the falling away, for *self* is to be then glorified. 262-24

As today ye come to those experiences of seeing, of feeling greater hope and love, greater peace and beauty, so rest ye in the Lord.

Oft hath He given, fret not thyself but stand still and see the glory of the Lord. These apply in thy experiences day by day. Keep in the way of the seeking—opening thy heart, thy mind for a greater service to others.

Teach thyself in teaching others to be patient, to be content; not satisfied but *content* in the ways of the Lord!

262-121

(Q) Why am I restless, unsettled?

(A) Not restless and unsettled in the inner self, but lack of response in the emotional body. Thus, keep self in accord. Ye chafe under duty, but do not that as would condemn self.

3282-1

(Q) Is it best to let this business proposal rest, or shall I try to force the issue?

(A) We would not *force* the issue, but we would not let it lag or rest! Rather put self in that position first physically *and* mentally to be able to meet or cope with, or to *advance* same—see? Then, as this is being accomplished, put self in the way of same being offered again—or the same proposal made both by self and from others.

279-1

24 / Rhythmic Return

 Like passing the winter solstice, you are passing the lowpoint and improvement will return naturally, with its own timing and rhythm. Here is a period to avoid ill-timed movement, while swelling one's awareness of the ebb and flow of all things. The time for action approaches; the inner resources are being recharged by the cosmic swing toward rebirth. One must be receptive and patient, not outgoing.

(Q) In view of present environment and conditions, would it be best to pull up stakes and go to Norfolk or vicinity, look for a job in any field to start with, and would this give opportunities for the opening of a Tea Room Luncheonette or Refreshment and Gas Service Station in this locality?

(A) If this is the desire, if this is what is wished, then pull up stakes and do it! This *must* be *determined* by *self!* It will *not* be given from here that you should hang *any* hope on *any* tree, on *any* place, on *any* thing, save on God—and let Him meet thee in self! as to *what* is the choice to be made, *ever,* by self.

Conditions may appear to be at the lowest ebb, but man and his own abilities must ever be eradicated if there will be the opportunity for the Creative Forces, the Creative Energies to work with same.   333-6

With the periods set aside for meditation—don't hurry yourself, don't be anxious but closing the self, the conscious mind to anxieties from without—enter within thine own inner temple. There let the voice, the feeling direct; yea, let the spirit of the purpose of self be free in its direction to self.   1861-18

The general resistance of the system we find at a lower ebb than we have had before at all. This is produced, as we see, through those physical conditions wherein the whole system is attacked through the forming of those poisons and bacilli, through the toxins as absorbed in the system, through uric acid that is taken back in system; and through the debilitation of the mental forces by *strain* in the mental and physical manner to the body.

As we see, for the best of the body physically and mentally, the body should *not ever* be in that condition that he *worries* over physical and mental *attitudes* toward conditions. 294-69

(Q) Any further advice for my better welfare?

(A) Go slow; or make haste slowly. Be patient with self and with others. Do not work self into a state of over-anxiety at the changes that will be found, or attempt to use up the strength and vitality mentally and physically to gain or maintain those balances that once were held in relationships to these; for these will come in their normal time. Forget not the source of thine inspiration in self, for they must be in the God of life, of truth, of hope, of love. 480-11

25 / Simple Purpose

Humans contrive to be many things that they are not, in order to build the ego's world. To manifest one's life artificially can lead only to ruin. To be oneself is to join nature's harmony, whereby one can, by one's very purity of being, give inspiration to others. By simplicity and clarity of purpose, one finds true meaning.

Thus these few, simple rules may apply in the experience of this entity:

First, ye must believe that God is. Thus ye may believe that He is a rewarder of those who diligently seek Him, in opening, in interpreting the experiences of the entity in this life to a more perfect understanding. Know there is the straight and narrow way. They who seek same may find Him, but there must be the application of self towards the ideals presented through those very impulses which brought this to bear in thy experience. Thus may it be summed up, as ye would that others should do to you, do ye even so to them. This is the law and the prophets.   3051-7

(Q) You have told me in my life reading [443-1] that I had many impulses. Will you now show me how to so harmonize them that my mind and emotions always work together?

(A) As may be seen by the experience of the entity, while the emotions and the impulses at times vary, this for many an individual—and for this body—is a natural manner of expression; and if the ideal is always kept as the measuring stick, as it may be termed, the developments will come in the natural order of things or experiences.

Hence in harmonizing, only let the impulses and the activities in those impulses be gauged by the ideal, and it will make for harmony in the experience of the entity in its development.   443-6

. . . there is seen in the make-up of human mentality that which seeks for the unknown, and this air; yet the simplicity of the ability of individuals to apply that as may be obtained from their own subconscious self, cosmic forces and universal consciousness (or call it by whatever name the individual may choose)—*this* is the great truth that *must* be apparent to the layman, the individual, the scientist, the mathematician, the historian, the individual seeking information through these sources finds this apparent.   254-46

Study then, first, the 14th, 15th, 16th and 17th of John. *Apply* them, as "This is Jesus speaking to [853]—*speaking!*"
What is thy answer? "I am ready, Lord." Or, "As soon as I get this done, I'll try."
These ye must answer within thyself.
For the will of each entity, of each soul, is that which individualizes it, that makes it aware of itself; and as to how this is used makes thee indeed a child of God.
He hath not willed that ye should perish, that ye should want, that ye would not know Him. What have *ye* willed? What is thy way? What is thy desire?
It becomes then so simple that the simplicity becomes the complexness of the daily life.   853-9

One must leave the sanctuary of her home and put to work the principles she espouses intellectually, or her life has little meaning. It strengthens one's faith to leave the securities of a familiar environment and face the world's tests. Expand horizons! Preparation for such forays should include inspirational teachings of those who have preceded, as this will build both humility and confidence.

(Q) Should I try and leave . . . [home] . . . for the summer, or next year, or both?

(A) That depends upon what has been determined, or is to be determined, in self, as to the various relationships and conditions as may surround the life. As has been seen, those prospects of leaving are well—in *many* of those changes that may come about. Accept these; but be sure—where there has been the ideal set—to remain first true to self, and thou will not be false to any! 369-9

Hence we find the influence in Jupiter with Neptune makes for the innate expressions or desires of the entity to be a rover, a wanderer as it were—yet seeking ever an expression, or that something which is latent or "just beyond" the horizon.

Such an attitude at times brings into the experience doubts and fears of others as respecting the entity's purpose, the entity's attitude towards the real abilities that are a portion of the entity's experience.   2331-1

As ye apply, as ye make use of that in hand, more is given thee. For, day unto day is sufficient, if use is made thereof; not to self, not to self alone. Not that self is not to be considered, but losing self in good is the better way to *find* self.

What is good? How is such defined in thy life—of awakening to all the possibilities that exist in thy intake of life and its phases? To do good is to think constructively, to think creatively. What is creative, what is constructive, ye may ask? That which never hinders, which never makes for the bringing of any harm to others.

1206-13

(Q) How could I bring about a more harmonious unity in my home in regard to my father and his wife, or would it be best at this time for me to leave their home?

(A) There must be first the quiet or harmony in one's own self if one would find harmony with the association with others. As we find, if we would have an alternative, not to remain away from home all the while, but portions of the time, it would be well.   1540-7

In considering the physical disturbances in the body, much more than the mere pathological conditions must be taken into consideration. While in the present this is not a mental condition, there may become such. But if proper precautions are taken and corrections made we should have an entirely new outlook on life, new abilities, new possibilities, new opportunities coming to this entity.   3392-1

27 / True Nourishment

 One's fundamental responsibility is to care for the body with right nourishment. True nourishment is that which furthers one's progress on the path. That which brings growth is what one should seek. What one ingests, be it food or thought, should not influence you to deviate from your goal.

Be oft in prayer, *oft* in meditation, *seeing* self gaining the proper nourishment, proper resuscitating forces from those elements being given to the system for its resuscitation.   2097-1

Then, as ye purpose in thy heart to do, let these first be thy considerations.

What *is* the ideal life? Let it be answered from each phase of thy experience. Ye find ye have a body, physical—with all its appetites, with all its desires, with its needs for food, with its needs for that with which it shall be clothed. Ye find a *mind*—ye *think,* ye act—this also is in need of food and of clothing. As ye clothe thy thoughts in words, are they in keeping with that as would bring thee blessings or a curse upon others?

Know that ye sow, that ye use as thy ideal, that alone may ye reap in thy experience.   1977-1

Life in its manifestation in an individual activity of an entity in the material world finds itself able, because of its very nature, to take from the food values, the emotions that arise in the mental body and its environment, that which—combined with the proper activity of that assimilated in the body—produces the sufficient elements for not only the resuscitation but the reconstruction of itself.   1068-1

(Q) How should the Lord's Prayer be used in this connection [verses keyed to spiritual centers in the body]?

(A) As in feeling, as it were, the flow of the meanings of each portion of same throughout the body-physical. For as there is the response to the mental representations of all of these in the *mental* body, it may build into the physical body in the manner as He, thy Lord, thy Brother, so well expressed in, "I have bread ye know not of."

281-29

Meditation is *emptying* self of all that hinders the creative forces from rising along the natural channels of the physical man to be disseminated through those centers and sources that create the activities of the physical, the mental, the spiritual man; properly done must make one *stronger* mentally, physically, for has it not been given? He went in the strength of that meat received for many days? Was it not given by Him who has shown us the Way, "I have had meat that ye know not of"? As we give out, so does the *whole* of man—physically and mentally become depleted, yet in entering into the silence, entering into the silence in meditation, with a clean hand, a clean body, a clean mind, we may receive that strength and power that fits each individual, each soul, for a greater activity in this material world.   281-13

28 / Courageously Bearing Weight

One may be required to bear more weight of circumstance than seems possible or fair. Strong pressures from outside bear down. Even when problems seem momentous and unsolvable, they need not crush you. Hold courageously and do not overreach in these times.

And His promises are sure; and that which ye receive, that *use!* For to have an ideal, for to have a purpose, for to have knowledge and understanding without the courage and the will to use same is to become a weakling, not worthy, not able above that doubt; even as Peter when he walked on the water.

And when you see the turmoils of the earth, and when you hear the cries of those that are fearful, and when you see the elements about thee apparently in destructive forces, and ye doubt—to be sure you sink into doubt and fear and despair; unless thy purpose is ever "Here am I, Lord, use me, direct me."   853-9

It is not in the tempest, not in the roar or the lore of the might of battle. Though there may be the destruction of life, of property (as is known materially)—no one can destroy the soul but self! *No one* but *self!*

God hath not willed that any soul should perish, but hath given even His Son, that brought even into the world that spirit of Christmas.

Let thy message be:

There *is* hope in Him. For there is the promise through, "Lo, I am with thee always, even unto the end of the world."

And though the world, the earth may pass away, though it may be burned up, though it may bring destruction to the material things, we look to Him, we know there is safety in Him.

Fear not he that may destroy the body, but rather fear him that may destroy the soul in torment. Then, in love, in obedience, in prayer, follow Him.   281-59

Each soul, as is known by the entity, enters an experience for the magnifying of the entity's ideal. For as has been given, He hath not willed that any soul should perish; neither does He seek to bring sorrow, disappointments, heartaches, in the experience of those activities in the earth—save it be for the edifying of the soul.

For whom the Lord loveth He chasteneth, and purgeth *every* one.   1466-3

Each soul as it has entered and does enter into material manifestation is to fulfill a purpose, with the Creative Forces or God. For He hath not willed that any soul should perish, but hath with every temptation, every fault, prepared a way, a manner, an opportunity for the entity to become as one with Him.

For that is the purpose of the soul's being in the beginning. Hence without beginning, without end.   257-201

29 / The Depths

In the depths of discouragement or despair, the hidden side of the soul is brought to bear. The sage does not panic but resorts to faith. In so doing the dark night becomes a welcome challenger and is turned into a creative force.

Will has influenced the entity *much* in this direction, and in the hours of greatest despair has come the light that is ever available when a body-entity allows the Divine—of which the soul is the spark, or portion—to enter in and make His abode there.   115-1

(Q) Is my health being affected by aggravation resulting from business association with my family, and would it be advisable to make a change?

(A) In part, as has been given! This comes from those—but it's more of a *physical*, else—those relationships with the family could be, and would be, made as stepping stones for *better* things, rather than being *allowed* to overcome and subdue the abilities!   279-1

(Q) Is the ill health which I have been experiencing the past years the result of mistakes of a past life or is it due to something amiss in this present life?

(A) Both. For there is the law of the material, there is the law of the mental, there is the law of the spiritual. That brought into materiality is first conceived in spirit. Hence as we have indicated, all illness is sin; not necessarily of the moment, as man counts time, but as a part of the whole experience. For God has not purposed or willed that any soul should perish, but purgeth everyone by illness, by prosperity, by hardships, by those things needed, in order to meet self—but in Him, by faith and works, are ye made every whit whole. 3395-2

Do not confuse self, do not overstep self, but as hath been said, "When ye call I will *hear*—and answer speedily."

This applies to thee—yea, to each soul, to be sure; but make it thine own cry, *with* the *willingness* in self to be led, to be guided, to be directed, by that as *He* hath given, "Ask in my name and ye—believing—shall have."

Can there be a greater promise? Oft ye, as so many, feel—or act—as if this meant someone else.

Is not thy soul as precious in His sight as though ye had taken a city, yea as though ye had directed a nation?

. . . In such meditation, then—in such may the self awaken to that strength of purpose, that *determination* to *carry on!* Though the world forsake thee, if thy Lord is upon thy side, ye stand even as Eleazar before the hosts of the Lord. [Num. 3:32] 165-26

30 / Sustaining the Fire

The mystery of fire permeates one's life. Its paradox of polarity is met at every turn: protector and destroyer. The fire is bright and active, yet depends on something dark and passive to sustain it. Your brightness and vitality captures notice, but be careful to also nurture the fuel—the dark partner that gives the fire's brightness the capacity to exist.

From Mars we find a tendency for the body-mind at times to be easily aroused to anger. Anger is correct, provided it is *governed*. For it is as material things in the earth that are not governed. There is *power* even in anger. He that is angry and sinneth not controls self. He that is angry and allows such to become the expression in the belittling of self, or the self-indulgence of self in any direction, brings to self those things that partake of the spirit of that which is the product or influence of anger itself.   361-4

In Mars with Uranus, beware that the temper does not overcome the better self; or beware of the associations that would make for the arising in the experience of those things when doubts respecting others bring an activity when wrath or madness, or tendencies in these directions, might bring destructive forces not only in this present experience but that which may make for development or retardment in the soul's sojourn also.

For, this is as the warning: Keep thine own *judgments*, yes. He that hath no temper is of little value, but he that controls not his temper is worse than though he had none at all!   524-1

We find from Mars that the entity has a very good temper; this isn't bad temper, but a *good* temper! One without a temper is in very bad shape, but one who can't control his temper is in still worse shape!   1857-2

Grit, or "get-up"—termed by many. This an element that may be both constructive and destructive in the make-up *of* an individual. Woe to him who may be *ruled* by wrath. Woe to him who is also of such a nature as to allow the temper, or the elements that make for impulses, to be so overshadowed by that as is *momentarily* necessary for the activities of a life and not grounded in Truth, that arises from *spiritual* concepts.   412-5

From the influences in Mars, as well as Jupiter, we find indicated rather anger or madness or wrath on the part of others more than of self. For while the entity has not gotten to where it is not able to be angry, we find that it has attained to that position where it may be angry and yet sin not.

But leave off rather those inclinations to hold grudges. Let such experiences be rather as not having been. *See* the light! For know, as ye may learn from the study of the motivative forces of mind, matter and spirit, if one but sets the face toward the light the shadows fall far behind.

        1695-1

31 / Unity Out of Tension

The conditions are auspicious for progress and achievement. Yet misfortune can result from being self-serving in motive. The sage is one who is always willing to listen to others' points of view and hence ensure their cooperation. Unity comes from your actions which subordinate your own power with sensitivity to those who have less.

Ye cannot sow selfishness and reap peace. Ye cannot sow selfishness or strife and reap that which brings harmony. Ye cannot be extravagant in thy words or thy activities and expect there to be always plenty in the activities or experiences of every nature.

Study, then, to show thyself approved, even as ye did in that experience as Mathias—to bring order out of chaos for *all*. Thus you will bring it for yourself also.

Thinkest thou that the love of the Father-God is for any individual above another? Be reminded that He is not a respecter of persons; and those who love Him keep His ways, and unto such will He be gracious.   1974-1

Then indeed there is no power that emanates that is not from God.

Then what is this Spirit of Rebellion, what is this Spirit of Hate? What is this Spirit of Self-Indulgence? What is this Spirit that makes men afraid?

Selfishness! Allowed, yes, of the Father. For, as given, He has not willed that the souls should perish but that we each should know the truth—and the truth would make us free. Of what? Selfishness!

Then we should each know that the sin which lies at our door is ever the sin of selfishness, self-glory, self-honor.

Hence as the Master has said, unless we become even as He, we may not in *any* wise enter in.   262-114

Think not that there is any shortcut to peace or harmony, save in correct living. Ye *cannot* go against thine own conscience and be at peace with thyself, thy home, thy neighbor, thy God! For as ye do it unto the least of thy brethren, ye do it unto thy Maker.   1901-1

Much may be lost through aggrandizement of selfish motives. Little of self is held in esteem above others, would there be humble and the contrite heart before the creative forces that give—give—to others that the understanding of relations between men as men, or man's relation to the creative forces—for in selfishness is the greatest plague, the greatest hindrance, the greatest barrier towards man's own development.   165-2

Be not overcome with those things that make for discouragements, for *He* will supply the strength. Lean upon the arm of the *Divine* within thee, giving not place to thoughts of vengeance or discouragements. Give not vent to those things that create prejudice. And, most of all, be *unselfish!* For selfishness is sin, before first thine self, then thine neighbor and thy God.

Love ye one another. Give as ye have received. 254-87

32 / Steadfast Endurance

To discover the continuity of life is a subtle art. The sage does not cling to the past or present, yet she finds a steady thread that weaves through life and connects each moment. If one is awake to the continuity of life, then it is a simple matter to endure calmly any challenge or concern.

Fear and the uses of same in thine experience maketh thee afraid. Let the knowledge of the Lord constrain thee day by day. Fear not those things of the flesh, of the body, that would hinder in thine understanding, thine knowledge of thy God. Though ye be in the midst of tempestuous forces of the earth, if the knowledge, if the love of the Christ be thy guide, ye will be strong, ye will be steadfast, ye will be patient   262-98

For, to the entity, it would require patience in these directions, and—as the teacher of old has given—"In patience possess ye your souls." This does not mean in bearing with individuals that willfully disobey, but rather being strong and steadfast and humble in the sight of higher forces, yet active in that known to be not only duty in the spiritual sense but duty in the mental and material sense. For, duty and patience are akin; for he that grows weary in well-doing, or who falters and faints and gives up, is not worthy of those things that may be his lot.   517-1

. . . where the treasure is the heart is also. Unless that as is determined in self is wholly in keeping with those precepts, those principles that may make for a continuity of life, hope itself, *little* may be expected. For, as given, this—here—in this place—now—may become as a shining light to many, or may become the laughingstock of many. 254-54

(Q) Please explain what was meant by seeking universal source as contact for helping self and others.
(A) Seeking the Spirit, or the *continuity* of life *within* self, which *is* the gift *of* the Creative Force in the experience of every entity! 267-1

Thus the using or applying of that as may be given will bring the better understanding, the better comprehension of the continuity of life and the application of the abilities in bringing into the experience of others that which will make for hopefulness in their experience.

For as each entity gains the understanding, more and more is there the realization that the purposes for which each soul enters any given experience are to apply the opportunities that are a part of the experience in bringing into the consciousness of others the fact of the continuity of life, and to bring hope and cheer. 622-4

33 / Retreat from Negativity

When inferior forces are intensifying, one only exhausts himself in attempting to subdue them head-on. It is better to yield ground and keep as free from contact with the onmoving negativity as is possible. Falling back is not giving in. Feel sure within yourself and your values, but step back and avoid battle. This is a time for introspection and patience.

(Q) Is it true, as I have felt, that I have enemies—those who are trying to do me out of my inheritance?

(A) Ye have no enemies. Let this ever be within thine own heart: Do *right* in self. And that which is thine own cannot, will not be taken from thee. Those who try such are enemies to themselves. Look not upon them as enemies to thee. Feel sorry for them for their misconstruction of right. 　　　　　　　　　　　3250-1

For what is bad? Good gone wrong, or something else? It is good *misapplied,* misconstrued, or used in a *selfish* manner—for the satisfying of a desire within self.

1089-5

(Q) How can she conduct herself so as to gain the goodwill and respect of her family and friends; and rid herself of her temper?

(A) As indicated, there must be builded the purposefulness in knowing self as one with constructive influences—that build for peace, harmony and happiness.

(Q) How should she be treated by her family?

(A) In that manner which may be called as loving indifference to the temperamental outbursts; not condemnation, but in that of quiet, peaceful contemplation with the body as to the manner in which the personality may be made for constructive influences or forces in the experience. 352-1

Learn ye patience, if ye would have an understanding, if ye would gain harmony and grace in this experience! "For in patience do ye possess your souls." It's when individuals have become impatient, and desire their own will or desire their expression or desire that they as individuals be heard, that they become less and less in that close association with the Divine—and more of that as is human and of the animal becomes manifest. This is a power, to be sure, but fraught with egotism becomes a destructive power.

And bad is only good gone wrong, or going away from God. 1201-2

Then only in *loving* indifference may the conditions be met.

What, ye say, is loving indifference?

Acting as if it had not been, save disregarding as if they were *not*. Not animosity; for this only breeds strife. Not anger; for this only will produce mentally and physically the disturbances that become as physical reactions that prevent meeting every phase of the experience; whether in the good, the hope, the help ye mete to others, or in keeping self—as has been given for self—unspotted from the *cares* of the world. 1402-2

34 / Resilient Strength

You have demonstrated your strength to bounce back from adversity or setback. Now, in a time of great personal power it especially behooves one to bear his ideals in mind. Do not abuse this influence and strength. When the cosmic flow is with one's every movement, there is the temptation to go beyond the limits of what is proper. The sage is one who does not forget his responsibility to the good, no matter how great his power waxes.

Hence in the present will come those experiences when, as a leader, as an officer even, the entity may be given power that may be exercised upon, and for or against, others; yet, used aright, may bring contentment—in the things that were as tenets then; used awrong, or as aggrandizing of self's own interests, *must* bring destructive forces in the experience of the entity.

329-1

With this entity then, as we find, the astrological influences make the entity naturally as one headstrong, as one naturally tended towards having its own way. Hence it depends upon the manners of usage of these tendencies as to whether they may become as forbearing or forgiving or for that oneness with Creative Forces, or for self-indulgences. Yet the entity is a natural leader, with the natural inclinations for directions that may be as an impelling influence, if not by might by power, if not by right by the main forces in associations itself.

Hence all the more reason that such an entity keep the ideal before self, not only of its material relationships, not only in the material positions, but more so in that the spiritual ideal is not lost sight of in all of the activity, in all of its relationships.   1211-1

In knowledge and power comes responsibility, that in patience may be tested in self. Be not overcome by either trials or by those joys that may make forgetfulness of the source from which the power comes. In patience is the race of life run, that the joys may be the greater in Him.   262-26

And if there will be first, in the present, the purposing and living in such a manner before God as to walk circumspectly in thine own conscience before Him, and in dealing as through that experience with thy fellow man, ye may find—as this world's goods increase in thy hands (as thy must necessarily do)—they will not and do not become burdens to thy conscience nor separate thee from thy home or thy fellow man. But rather is the opportunity to serve thy Maker.
Ye have earned that right for much of this world's goods. Do not abuse that; else ye become—in thine *own* conscience—an outcast in this experience.   1901-1

So as ye come to thine weakness, find thine strength and thine power and thine love in Him; and life's pathways will grow brighter, though the road may be rough, though there may be words that are harsh. Yet as thou lookest upon that tower of strength in thine seal as of the pyramid, as thou reliest upon the cross of Him who bore it for thee, the rose of love, light and radiance will bear thee up, and thou wilt not dash thy foot against a stone.
          845-1

Here is a time when forward movement is easily possible. It is a time for you to thrive in the full light of the sun. Opportunities to prosper are before you now. Attention to one's duties and the extension of one's spiritual path are the keys to successful usage of this opportune time.

It is not the knowledge, then, but what one does with one's abilities, one's opportunities in relationships to others, that makes for the development or retardment of that individual.   1293-1

From those things given as to the experiences and application of self, it may be seen that knowledge alone does not make one wise. With the abilities to use that thou hast in hand may there come understanding. 540-1

It is well to gain that full concept that all there is in materiality is of the spirit; is of the spirit of truth, if it is constructive. They that live by the spirit, through the mental attributes of same, shall prosper in the Lord. They that live by might or main, though their days may be glamorous, find that contentment shall flee away; and those things that make for disorder, disturbance, distrust, must arise in the experience, for these are not the fruits of the spirit. For these are they: Just being kind, just being in that manner in which the fellow man is served day by day; and that the outcome of same is fellowship, patience, kindness, gentleness, brotherly love—these manifested in the experience; not by jerks and spurts but as a living example day by day, not to be seen of men alone but rather that which is done in secret shall be proclaimed from the housetops.   391-8

(Q) Will this firm be successful and prosper?
(A) As has been indicated, as we find so long as there is the holding to the ideals of each, it will be successful.

877-17

In seeking to know that opportunity that is given each in the present, it is one thing to live that there may be presented to another that which will open another's opportunity; and it is for *self* to recognize and use the opportunity in self's own development.

But know, as each has been called, that there will come the *greater* opportunity in self's development, self's understanding, in preparing that which is for the enlightenment of thine neighbor.

262-50

In that which has been thus far presented, each individual in its own way is finding the consciousness of opportunity. And the lessons that may be presented from such individuals may be made worthwhile in the experience of those who seek to understand opportunity from the view that has been presented, in that opportunity itself—of the spiritual activity in the experience of individuals—comes to materialization in what the individual does respecting that the individual holds as the spiritual activity of such an experience as related to *its* ideal.

262-51

When circumstances prevent progress, even threatening one's ultimate continuation toward the goal, one does best to draw the light of her spiritual foundations within herself, to preserve it from harm. It is the warmth and constancy of this light which helps one to persevere in adversity, and to avoid the strong forces which attempt to turn her from her way.

They that endure unto the end shall wear a crown of life. They that persevere shall overcome. *He* should be, and is, thy guide and thy light, and thy strength—if ye will trust in Him.

Viewed from the material sojourn, apparently every hopeful endeavor, every hopeful period of the entity's sojourn during this experience has been shattered either by seemingly unnecessary disappointments or by forebodings that have become at times as obsessions.

Yet the determination to go on, to do and to be, has driven and does drive the entity at all times. And it would never, under any circumstance, do for this entity—now—in the present experience—to do other than to be striving onward always.   1816-1

Now we find these are improving, and only needs keep on keeping on, until we will bring the desired results, for this will prove a successful operation. Then, give as this: Conditions on improve. Best push forward, and do not be discouraged. Success is coming.   4905-14

(Q) Please give me any other advice I may need at present.

(A) Do not allow disturbing conditions to so *fret* the

body-physical as to undermine or to sap the vitality. *Know,* as has oft been given, in thine own *strength alone* little may be accomplished, but in the strength of the power and the might of thine Savior, in and through His promises, *much* may be done. 303-13

And do find patience with self. It has been said, "Have we not piped all the day long and no one has answered?" Seekest thou, as was given from this illustration, for the gratifying of thy self? or seekest thou to be a channel of blessing to thy fellow man? They may not have answered as *thou* hast seen. They may have even shown contempt, as sneering, for thy patience and thy trouble. But *somewhere* the sun still shines; *somewhere* the day is done; for those that have grown weary, for those that have given up. The Lord abhorreth the quitter. And those temptations that come in such cases are the viewing of thine own self. Ye have hurt thyself and ye have again crucified thy Lord, when ye become impatient or speak harshly because someone has jeered or because someone has sneered or because someone has laughed at thy efforts!

Leave the *results* leave the giving of the crown, leave the glory, with the Lord! *He* will repay! Thou sayest in thine own heart that thou believest. Then merely, simply, *act* that way! In speech, in thought, in deed. 518-2

37 / Working Together

The creation of harmony depends upon each of those involved fulfilling his function, attending to his responsibilties. Only then does purposeful, mutual work shape a familylike atmosphere. Words mean little unless they are supported by complementary action that forges common bonds. Then the words have reality and truth in them.

But make for ever the companionableness, so that there may ever be the seeking by the developing mind for counsel, for guidance; and for the answering of why the thoughts arise under various circumstances as to conditions in the physical body, the physical relationships, the mental activities and the mental reactions.

For to keep such is to give and to be in the position of *fulfilling* the purposes whereunto one is dependent upon the other.

For it is a unison of desire that brings a seeking at any time for expression, and *not* in *combative* reactions at all! For when there is the combative self-assertion, egotism and selfishness rise to the forefront *as* that ordinarily known as self-protection—which is a first law.

But as long as there is kept that unison, correct—as long as there is that *great* activity which all should know. If the world will ever know its best, it must learn *cooperation!*   759-13

(Q) Is there anything I can do to bring about a more friendly relationship between my parents and myself and family?

(A) This condition enters into many varying relationships. The causes which are to some unreasonable; to others of a very definite nature. That which is to the body, individual, an irritation, may be overcome. That as is held as animosity in the eyes of others must be overcome within themselves. *Satisfy* self that the proper attitude is being taken by self as regarding the relationships, considering that *others* have the right of *their* opinion as well as self, and an amiable condition may be arrived at, one more satisfactory than existent at present. Yet, as to what the actions of *others* are may not be governed by the individual, other than *self's* own action as respecting same.

2744-2

As has been given of old, "Take that thou hast in hand." Use same day by day. And as that ye use, as that ye know is applied in those directions, those principles as indicated, in the home, in the daily labors, in the daily associations, social, material and otherwise, then that as is necessary for the next step is given.   633-5

... for, as in individual life, more and more must there be the necessity of business and business relations on every hand to have an ideal. The sooner the necessity is recognized in the minds, the hearts, the souls of individuals that carry on *in* the commercial or business world, the sooner will there come that regeneration which will make for the drawing together of those who may make the day of the Lord at hand; for in Him we live and move and *have* our being. Business must have an ideal, a soul.   257-88

38 / Polarity

 In spite of an underlying oneness, nevertheless your life is shaped by the mix and flux of polarizing forces: yin and yang, dark and light, pessimistic and optimistic. The sage discerns clearly how things that are fundamentally connected still should not join. Skillfully put the elements of your life into creative opposition while acknowledging the essential link.

(Q) Please explain the existence of darkness before the existence of light.

(A) . . . He has not willed that any soul should perish, but from the beginning has prepared a way of escape! What, then, is the meaning of the separation? Bringing into being the various phases that the soul may find in its manifested forms the consciousness and awareness of its separation, and itself, by that through which it passes in all the various spheres of its awareness. Hence the separation, and light and darkness. Darkness, that it had separated—that a soul had separated itself from the light. Hence He called into being Light, that the awareness began. Hence we look out and see the heavens, the stars; and, as the psalmist has said: "The heavens declare the glory of God and the firmament sheweth his handiwork, as day unto day uttereth speech and night unto night sheweth knowledge" . . .

(Q) [288]: Is it true that day and night are condensed or miniature copies of incarnations into the earth and into planetary or spiritual sojourns; they in turn being miniature copies of what took place in the beginning?

(A) Very good, if you understood just what all this means! It's a very good illustration of that which has just been given; as to how there is the evolution of the soul, evolution of the mind, but not evolution of matter—save through mind, and that which builds same . . .

(Q) [295]: May I have a message on Day and Night that will help me in my contribution to the lesson?
(A) *Think* on the experiences of self, as self has passed from darkness unto light, from day unto night, in the *mental* associations of that which makes the awareness of that which would make of thee a channel of blessings to many. And then there may be seen in self's experience the meaning of what is Day, and what is Night. The ability to become aware; or, to put into other words, to become *conscious* is Day and Night . . .

(Q) [379]: May I have a message that will help me in contributing to the lesson?
(A) In self's own physical self there may be the illustration of Day and Night. Each element, each corpuscle of the body is a universe in itself, or a universe on the beginning of power and force. When there is that called disease, there becomes the unawareness or the darkness—of the light that may become Life in its manifested form. So, from Day and Night gain this lesson: Only in the experiencing of that which is the awareness of same may we know *what* is Day and Night.   262-56

39 / Small Progress

 Any dramatic progress is ill-advised here because your situation is weak and afflicted. It is time for one to reaffirm contact with his spiritual source and to eschew any distant goals. The sage refuses to overreach and instead sets little goals that are within reach. Progress can be made, even if it is limping movements hampered by restraints.

Then follow rather in the footsteps of the Messenger, or the Prince of Peace, that met each circumstance, or took those steps by steps as were necessary for the advancement to that position that all came to be in the active forces of the body. So, as with this body, step by step, meet those conditions as arise, either in the physical, the mental or the spiritual plane, in their order.   294-136

For each cell is as a representative of a universe in itself. Then what would ye do with thy abilities? As ye give to others, not hating them, to know more of the Universal Forces, so may ye have the more, for, God is love.

Do that, and ye will bring bettered conditions for yourself. Work where you are. As was given to those who were called, "The ground upon which ye stand is holy." Begin where you are.   4021-1

(Q) How can I use my energy to get the most out of life?

(A) In understanding or listening to those voices that speak from within and about self. Not material; but those *unseen* sources are *opening* to the abilities. Apply; do not abuse. Rather harken to that still small voice; for know that while the storms may—in all their picturesque beauty—bring fears or joy in the hearts of many, and that the ravages of war and the boldness as created by the spirit of patriotic influences are aroused, these are *outward* signs—and that which *builds* is the still small voice from within. Seek not "Who shall ascend into the heavens to bring him down, or go to the ends of the earth that ye may know!" Rather that that is within thine own self only needs the line upon line, the line upon line, to bring the understanding that *He lives*—and all is well! 2741-1

This, then, is as a lesson to the entity, that in the taking on of that experience that the entity sees, knows, understands, grasps a portion of, in the various phases of its earthly or physical or material existence, the lessons are then as stepping-stones, and *wade* in, rather than dive in head first. For little by little, line upon line, line upon line, must one gain the full concept of the conditions in which one lives, moves, and has its being. Not that life and its phases are a mystery, or something to be afraid of, but rather that the glory of the knowing *of* the existence and its *meaning* is the worthwhile condition in the material and the spiritual spheres and planes.

137-84

40 / Forgiving Release

 The sage is forgiving of inferior behavior by those around her when her freedom to progress is restored. In one's own liberation to move ahead once again, there is also a willingness to let go and forgive others who have been a source of constraint. The danger or the threat is gone, and now comes the time to move ahead with one's newfound freedom and release the past.

But learn that lesson—if ye would be loved, show thyself lovely; if ye would have friends, show thyself friendly; if ye would not be persecuted or talked about, then do not talk about others; if ye would have forgiveness, then forgive—even as ye would be forgiven.

These are not merely as theorems or theses for the contemplation, but are practical, applicable experiences in the manners of the affairs and associations of each individual, if they will but be applied in the experience.

2271-1

(Q) How can I overcome antagonistic forces in self and others?

(A) By *actual* manifesting forgiveness, more and more. As has been given, "Is it easier, Son, thy sins be forgiven, or to say Arise, take up thy bed and walk? but *that ye may know* that the Son hath power to *forgive*" [Matt. 9:5-6]— meaning to forget the weakness and give *strength* to those that falter. Even so, in overcoming antagonistic feelings, forgive as ye would *be* forgiven, remembering then no more. This overcomes antagonism and antagonistic influences; for as self *was, is,* an influence *in* dispersing *feelings* in hearts and souls of peoples, the thoughts held create the currents upon which the wings of experience must pass, and then—as these are made in positive contacts—so does antagonism be overcome, love made manifest, glorying in thine own ability *in* Him; not in self, *in* Him! 538-30

As ye would have mercy shown thee, ye show mercy to those that even despitefully use thee. If ye would be forgiven for that which is contrary to thy own purposes—yet through the vicissitudes of the experiences about thee, anger and wrath give place to better judgment—ye, too, will forgive those that have despitefully used thee; ye will hold no malice. For ye would that thy Ideal, that Way ye seek, hold no malice—yea, no judgment—against thee . . .

Hence as ye give, ye receive. For this is mercy, this is grace. This is the beauty of the inner life lived. 987-4

In showing forth that which is manifest in thine experience, let the love that was manifested in forgiveness be in thee, that there be no envy, no strife, no knowledge of other than good works through the activities of self. For, in glorying in the knowledge of the Father comes more and more the manifestations of the Spirit of the Christ. "Inasmuch as ye do it unto the least of these, my little ones, ye do it unto me." 262-47

41 / Decrease

What has played a large role in your life will now diminish. However, there is not cause for worry. Times of gain are naturally followed by times of decrease or loss. Use this period to diminish your involvements, to return to basic values. Respect simplicity and quietude. This is an interim period of rest and outward inaction.

(Q) What other advice should I now have, step by step, to rebuild myself, faith in myself and my future?

(A) This is rather *out* of the question under the present situation. Conditions are to arise, naturally, through such activities, that are to be both troublesome and disconcerting; in any attempt to rebuild . . .

We do not begin to build before the situation is *cleared.*

This, then, is step by step: First *clear* the situation; allowing sufficient time to elapse to prevent this being forced to be reopened again . . .   257-122

Then what is the real problem?

Hold fast to that as ye purpose in thy heart, that there *will* be the opportunity for those that are through their own shortcomings losing, or have lost, sight of their relationships.

Then put on rather the whole armor. Look within self, first. Clear that doubt of thy association, thy connection with that divine source, that *with* which ye may conquer *all*; and *without* which even all the fame, all the fortune of the age would not bring that ye have purposed to do into the experience of even *one* soul—the relationship of the soul to its Maker and the Maker's relationship to that created!

. . . But whom the Lord would exalt, He first brings low that they may know the strength is of the Lord—and not in hosts but the still small voice that beareth witness with thy soul, thy spirit, that ye walk that straight and narrow way that leadeth to understanding. And in saving those of thy own shortcomings, ye find ye have been lifted up.

165-26

In those forces from the activities or sojourns in the *extreme* or the Uranian influence, we find great stresses and great strains; experiences when the entity finds itself very enthusiastic, and others when *everything* seems or appears to be at a very low ebb.

These extremes are to be watched. Rather than using them as stumbling stones, make of the stepping-stones.

For the hope and faith and patience and long-suffering, gentleness and kindness as may be manifested to others, will bring into the experience peace and contentment that may not be found in the great emotions without the serious considerations of all phases of an experience; or even in the great stresses when the entity would tend to make great sacrifices of one nature or another, whether in things pertaining to the ideals or just the outlook as to what people will say.

1530-1

42 / Applying the Will

During a time of upswing, the sage uses the growing forces to improve self, making right choices to purge self of the inferior aspects of personality, and following the patterns of right thinking. The sage knows that at such a propitious time, good decisions make possible the achievement of great progress.

(Q) Are hereditary, environment and will equal factors in aiding or retarding the entity's development?

(A) Will is the greater factor, for it may overcome any or all of the others; provided that will is made one with the pattern, see? For, no influence of heredity, environment or whatnot, surpasses the will; else why would there have been that pattern shown in which the individual soul, no matter how far astray it may have gone, may enter with Him into the holy of holies?   5749-14

Then, there is the will of the creative forces and the purposes for which each soul or entity enters an experience. For He hath not willed that any soul should perish, but has with every temptation prepared a way, a means not only of escape but of turning that which may appear to be a physical conflict into greater channels for manifestation of the glorifying of the name of the Father, the Son—*through* the application of self in its relationships to its opportunities and conditions that present themselves in the experience of an entity.   1947-1

Then, when these are weighed, choose thou. For, as has ever been, there is no influence that may supersede the will of man; for such are the gifts unto the sons of men that they may make their souls such as to be the companionship with the All-Wise, All-Creative Forces, or separate from them. For, there is no impelling force other than that, "If ye will be my people, I will be your God." 440-16

For the will of each entity, of each soul, is that which individualizes it, that makes it aware of itself; and as to how this is used makes thee indeed a child of God.

He hath not willed that ye should perish, that ye should want, that ye would not know Him. What have *ye* willed? What is thy way? What is thy desire?

It becomes then so simple that the simplicity becomes the complexness of the daily life. 853-9

As to what an entity does concerning its environs or hereditary influence from the *material* viewpoint, this is governed by the action of the will (that active principle making for the *individuality* of an entity, from those atomic forces that may manifest in a material plane or in *any* sphere of material or matter existence). Thus is *man* endowed with the individual soul.

Hence the *will* is an *attribute* of the soul, and the whole development of an entity. 274-1

43 / Resolute Breakthrough

Opposing forces are at an ebb. With resolute action take advantage of these times to make a breakthrough. Nonviolently, but with firm resolve, press ahead. Be unwavering to your highest principles and exhibit honesty to yourself and others. Resolute consistency turns the tide.

As to those conditions about the body, the relationships and those activities pertaining to success:

Look not upon that which *has* been. Remember, he that looketh back is as one bereft of the reasons that would make for the activities. If the success is to be put to the same usages that it was when accomplished in the past, what good would same be in thine experience?

Such material things should be looked forward to, then rather in the manners as we have oft indicated. Be not unmindful that consistency in speech, in act, in the relationships to thy neighbor, in *every* way becometh one. And rather let those things that have been be forgotten. Build upon those things worthwhile, but look not back.   257-155

Hence one of those influences which should ever be first and foremost is consistency, as well as persistency.

And know that the ideals must ever be of a constructive, creative nature, if there is to be harmony, peace, or even a semblance of material success.   2160-1

(Q) What general advice may be offered to me for my personal guidance in making myself successful both in the eyes of God and man?

(A) Keep those policies that have builded self to know self to be honest with self. And when you are honest with self you will not be false to the God or to the fellow man.

Meet every condition fairly, squarely. Every act must be met by self, in its dealings with its fellow man. 335-4

The answers, then, are within thyself. For thy body is indeed the temple of the living God. There He has promised to meet thee, in the holy of holies—thy purpose, thy will.

Will ye make it then to be at-one with His purpose? Let thy prayer ever be:

"*Lord, have Thine own way with me!Use me in the way and manner Thou seest, O God, that I may be the greater channel of blessings to others, to glorify Thee—here and anow!*"

That is the attitude, my friend, that will bring thee closer and yet closer to the knowledge, the understanding and—yea—with same the wisdom to apply that thou knowest.

He asketh not that ye apply that ye know not of, but desires that every soul "Seek and ye shall find, knock and it will be opened unto thee."

These are not merely sayings, beautiful to hear yet impractical in daily life! Have ye not observed and found that these are in keeping with the law?   2524-3

44 / Avoiding Evil

If one allows evil to become a part of her life, so that she is accustomed to its presence, she will fall under its power eventually. Evil cannot survive the cosmic unity of the sage, who makes plain her intentions to continue on the path and to eschew that which is less than beneficial to that end.

Which is the more real, the love manifested in the Son, the Savior, for His brethren, or the essence of love that may be seen even in the vilest of passion? They are one. But that they bring into being in a materialized form is what elements of the one source have been combined to produce a materialization. Beautiful, isn't it?

How far, then, is ungodliness from godliness? Just under, that's all!   254-68

(Q) How can I rise above my last period of depression and feel that I am going forward again?

(A) Set thine thoughts and thine mind on things that pertain to His love, His will, and those things that would hinder become as the shadows in the background, and look not upon that in the rear . . .

(Q) Were evil forces warring within me, or was it my reasoning mind that caused this depression?

(A) As has been given from the beginning, "There is set before thee good and evil. Choose thou." In the choosing, in the setting of thine will in that direction or the other direction allows those influences to become magnified or lessened by that in the promises.   288-30

What, then, ye may ask, *is* the will of the Father here, now, under the varying circumstances that ye confront in the present? with thy problems that are thine heritage through the use thou hast made, and are making in thy dealings with thy fellow man day by day.

To do good, to eschew evil, to love mercy and judgment, saith the prophet, is the whole duty of man—as related to his activities in the earth. 2524-3

Love mercy and justice, eschew evil; and keep thy heart *singing* all the while. For the joy of the service in the love of the Lord maketh the heart glad. Look not upon those things that make for disturbing influences, as of an evil force. For God so *loved* the world as to give His Son, that we through Him might know *eternal* life! 262-116

As ye then forgive those who trespass, who speak evil, who are ungentle, who are unkind, so may the Father forgive thee when thou art wayward, when *thou* art headstrong and seek His face . . .

Then, if thou wouldst know what may be the understanding heart, just be kind, just be patient, just be lovely, just be friendly to thy fellow man. *Forgive* those that speak lightly or unkindly, or who even in premeditated manner do thee evil. For if ye forgive not these, how can thy heavenly Father forgive thee? 792-1

45 / Harmonious Gathering

Trust a force beyond your knowledge which is drawing you and others together. It is a time for collecting and assemblinng people with a common feeling or a shared vision. A strong center radiates a harmonious group and creates accord. Discover the true source of the cohesive force between people.

First, as has been oft given, there is *strength* in unity of purpose—for, as has been given, "Where two or three gather together in my name, I am in the midst of same," and if in that name ye ask *believing* ye shall receive according to the faith that lies within each and every one of you; for God is not mocked, and whatsoever ye sow, so shall ye reap. As ye build, so shall the *structure* be.

254-52

(Q) [689]: How is the best way to cooperate with other organizations who are in sympathy with or who have an understanding of this work?

(A) As has so oft been given. Let those that are sincere, that are honest with themselves, seek not the differences in the organizations but where they may cooperate. And as they do, you will find—as with these that are gathered here, they are of many faiths, many creeds, yet they find one common purpose—*good* to thy fellow man! So, as those that have found in this vision, in this interpretation, or in that promotion or in that experience of this or that nature, seek rather the common interest where there *is* cooperation, rather than the differences. And then if any group, if any organization, if any association has not this, it has not the full soul.

254-95

For if ye would in thy daily or material life be a musician, may ye think of thy music once a week or a month or a year? or art thou making it a portion *of* thy *life?*

If ye would be an athlete, would ye disregard thy hours, thy body, thy meals? or would ye work *at* that which ye would make as a portion of thy real inner self?

Are thy relationships, thy friendships, such that ye need only to mention or to speak of or to act *at* or like there is never any communication with same? or are they renewed, with the memory of those periods when thou wert enjoined one with another, in a common purpose, in a oneness of desire?   281-26

There may be different channels of approach, yes. For not all peoples walked in the field when the wheat was ripe. Neither did all stand at the tomb when Lazarus was called forth. Neither were they all present when He walked on the water, nor when He fed the five thousand, nor when He hung on the cross. Yet each experience answered, and does answer to something within each individual soul-entity. For each soul is a corpuscle in the body of God. And when differences arise in a body, where corpuscles are at variance to a common purpose for all, sin enters, and death by sin, to whatever may be that group, that organization, that is stressing differences rather than the coordinating channels through which all may come to the knowledge of God.   3395-2

46 / Ascending

 It is through the consistency of will and attention that the sage builds toward the goal. Using every small action in an important way, she rises to a higher level. Nothing happens automatically, but this is a positive time, and one should ascend confidently and deliberately, while maintaining a keen awareness of what she is building.

(Q) Any other advice or counsel for the body?
(A) Build on as thou hast started. Keep thine face towards the light, and the shadows will be in the background. Turn not upon those things that would become an undoing, but press onward—upward—ever!   369-9

. . . to succeed the body must press ever onward, upward, and the new construction may be met with fears, yet gives the open way and a clear understanding of those truths as are gained by the ascending of the mountain.   900-34

In the uses then to which this entity may use these forces and understanding, be not fainthearted whether from physical or financial disability. Ever pressing onward, upward, relying wholly on Him who has made the way, the path, to the everlasting, and through the will, bring to submission all those conditions that would, through selfishness or desire, destroy the better elements within self, looking to that city without foundation whose builder and maker is God.   3791-1

Then, let the entity gain that as the first the knowledge of self, and of Him who gives all good and perfect gifts, then the ever-correcting force of His purpose, as is in

Him, be directed in that channel, leading then ever upward, onward, to that bright and holy land.   487-4

As there is put into activity that gained, and as self looks onward, upward, there comes the clarifying of the way in the consciousness of self. There *is* the growth in self. Be not weary in well-doing.   262-30

In the uses then to which this entity may use these forces and understanding, be not fainthearted whether from physical or financial disability. Ever pressing onward, upward, relying wholly on Him who has made the way, the path, to the everlasting, and through the will, bring to submission all those conditions that would, through selfishness or desire, destroy the better elements within self, looking to that city without foundation whose builder and maker is God.   3791-1

Thus may the entity, if it will but look within the heart of self, know that the study of self, the study of self's purposes, and analyzing same in the light of the Master Jesus, may enable one to find the beauty of love, the joy of love, the joy of living in the past and in the present. But look ever upward, onward, to that new day in which all will come before the throne of grace and mercy.   3954-1

47 / Confinement

You have been ensnared and limited by a mistaken perspective on life. Misplaced trust creates restriction and distress. Although the cycle has swung away from outward progress, the sage waits quietly and keeps firm in the face of repression or confinement.

(Q) Was the experience that I have gone through necessary?

(A) Unless the entity, unless the body looks upon the experiences day by day as necessary influences and forces, and uses them as a stepping-stone, soon does life become a pessimistic outlook. If each and every disappointment, each and every condition that arises, is used as a stepping-stone for better things and looking for it and expecting it, then there will still be continued the optimism. Or the looking for and expecting of. If an individual doesn't expect great things of God, he has a very poor God, hasn't he?   462-10

(Q) In regard to the entity's life reading [295-1], just what is it that is innate in the entity that would lead to unhappiness in marriage?

(A) Mistrust of men!

(Q) Does this mean the entity should never consider marriage in this life, but go through life never expecting to have a home of her own, for which she has yearned since a child?

(A) Be well to choose, or to take that one—if she so desires—and bear the consequences! Make her a bigger and a better woman! but those conditions as we have outlined are as we have seen them!

(Q) How can the entity best overcome the loneliness that so often besets her?

(A) Fill the life with the interests of others, and not so much of self—or belittle self, or condemn self for the conditions. Fill the life in the interests of others.   295-2

But leave out of thy thought those things which have too often become as barriers in thy gaining thy proper understandings. Do not complain as to the "bad luck" that has come, or that appears to be. Do not blame others, or any influence. Rather meet such in Him.   1816-1

(Q) Any message for the group as a whole?
(A) Be ye joyous in thy service to thy fellow man, in the *name* of Him who is able to keep thy ways. Count thy hardships, thy troubles, even thy disappointments, rather as stepping-stones to know His way better. Be ye joyous; be ye happy in *His love.* For He hath loved us, even when afar. How much more when we try, though we may stumble and fail! For the trial, the test, the *determination* creates that which will rise as faithful, true, and as righteousness before the throne of grace. For thou art under a dispensation of mercy. Be ye merciful. Be ye unhurt by hard words.   262-83

48 / Wellspring

Lifewaters arise from the depths. The ubiquitous and nourishing source of life flows through you to those in need. Maintain your access to the central source of knowledge in order to be a blessing to the many.

Build not a one-sided life, knowing that he that is well-grounded is as a tree planted by the waters of life, that that given out is as for the healings of many—whether in those of the mental forces or those of material gains of life; and let not thine physical endeavors be evil-spoken of. 1727-1

Then, turn to thine own opportunity within to know Him while it is yet day in thine own material consciousness. Sow the seeds of truth, of brotherly love, of kindness, of gentleness, of patience. And know, that alone ye possess is that which ye have *given away!* That which ye command or demand is never a defense, but rather a judgment ye have set upon thine own self.

Then, let thy well [wellspring? Pr. 16:22; 18:4] be renewed within thee, that ye may show forth in the days of thy awareness as to thy relationship to thy brother, that ye take thought of him in that as ye would have men do to you, ye do even so to them. 1759-1

There *have* been periods when the entity, through various forms or manners of seeking, has touched—yea, for the moment opened—the wellspring of understanding. And then through infinite mysteries these have at times been shattered by the mysteries of the experiences in associations with others.

The desire, the hope in the present is to use self, self's abilities, for the awakening of hope, the arousing of faith to activity. And this is bringing that peace, that hope within the experience of self that is making this experience to become as it were the greater of all the experiences of the entity through the sojourns in the earth.

1613-1

For all power *has* been given unto *Him* who hath overcome the world, overcome even death; and is at the right hand of glory; that we, too, may know the way, the light; that we may drink *deep* of the waters of life . . .

540-3

(Q) How can she broaden her social life?
(A) In the same way and manner. Be a *source* of knowledge to all, and this attracts those not only whom the entity may help but who may aid the entity—in all fields of activity that have to do with mental, material and spiritual development.
(Q) What will bring back the entity's zest and love of life?
(A) Engaging in, and aiding others in, same.   189-3

49 / Timely Change

The time draws near for radical change in the way you present yourself to the world. Like an animal that sheds its skin in due season, your new self is ready to come forth. If you try to remain stable on what has been solid in the past, you will lose your equilibrium. Accept the disruptions before you now as purposeful, creative revolution.

(Q) Any advice regarding the world changes beginning June 25th, as they might affect my husband and me; also as to the attitude for us to hold?

(A) . . . The attitude of all should be:

"*Thy will be done, O God! And let me find myself content with that I cannot change, and to change that which I may that will be in closer keeping with Thee.*"   1100-37

(Q) Give the body any advice and counsel that will help him at this time.

(A) Has the body determined in self that it has chosen wisely and well in its activities day by day? In its choice of association in every direction, are they in keeping with the ideal the body has sought, does seek, and in taking such stock of self the body will find *some* changes, *some* conditions that amendments or change will be gradually brought about. Think not to destroy anything by the merely quitting or changing of same, until a whole consciousness is gained of the *purpose* of it all. Do not fight blindly or in the dark, for the whole of the physical and mental training of the body has been—and is—of a purpose, or a reason for accomplishing or going about any activity. Then, are those activities—are those purposes—in accord with the ideal as is builded, as is sought, as may be *found by* the self? Then work like thunder!   99-7

It is also understood, comprehended by some, that a new order of conditions is to arise; that there must be many a purging in high places as well as low; that there must be the greater consideration of each individual, each soul being his brother's keeper.

There will then come about those circumstances in the political, the economic and the whole relationships where there will be a leveling—or a greater comprehension of this need.

For as the time or the period draws near for these changes that come with the new order, it behooves all of those who have an ideal—as individuals, as well as groups or societies or organizations, to be practicing, applying same in their experience—and their relationships as one to another.

For unless these are up and doing, then there must indeed be a new order in *their* relationships and their activities.

For His ways will carry through. For as He gave, "Though the heavens and the earth may pass away, my word will *not* pass away."

All too often has this message been forgotten in the pulpits and in the organizations, not only in the national relationships but in the international relationships.

3976-18

50 / Vessel

Order comes from harmony between two sides of life. To be a fit vessel for the Spirit, your material life must be balanced with your spiritual life. Only then can peace of mind and true prosperity flow into your life. You are like a great vessel that is used to cook and serve nourishing food and also to offer ritual sacrifice to the heavens.

For as there is made manifest in the life, the activity, the giving of such a vessel as this into the experiences of man, there should be the realization more and more—in the hearts and minds of all who come in contact with the entity—that God, the Father, keeps His promises to the children of men; giving them those vessels, those channels, through which *hope* and faith, and patience, are made manifest. 2156-1

Who hath said what manner of vessel this shall be? The Lord is the potter, *we* are the clay! Would *we*, then, say what manner of man we should be? Rather being a *vessel* of the Lord, and *used* by Him as a vessel for service in whatsoever field He has chosen we should go! Kick not against thine lot, nor against those things that beset thee in thine disappointments in men, or their relationships as one to another. Knowest thou not they, too, are vessels of Him that rules over all? 539-1

Hence hold fast to that thou hast gained. For as given, thy prayers are heard. Thou art a chosen vessel, thou knowest the way. As to attempt to guide or as to how, hold *fast* to that which is good. *Hold fast* to that faith, that blessing He hath given. Even as thou hast seen thy Lord, may His blessings ever be as these:

"They that love me, they that keep my commandments—they are not grievous to bear, for they bring *rest* not to body but to thy soul."   1301-1

... for the light is set in Him, and thou art chosen as a vessel for that light. Be not broken on the wheel of strife, nor yet be thou overanxious—for these are but the wayside of those who would be led astray. Keep the counsel of Him who gave that, "Come unto me and I will make thy burden light, for my yoke is easy—but learn of me."
                                                                      254-35

(Q) Are we using the correct methods of breathing and intonation in our group meditations?

(A) As has been given in Meditation, to some, *this* then is the correct manner: As has been given so oft of old, purge ye your bodies, washing them with water, putting away those things of the mind and of the body; for tomorrow the Lord would speak with thee.

Hence in this group make thy mind, thy body, as a fit subject for a visit of thy Lord, thy God.   281-28

51 / Trial

When a sudden change of events brings shock and upheaval into the life of the sage, his reaction is to examine himself and his actions, lest he behave in a faithless way. It is the internal self that is at stake, and one must learn to remain calm in the face of the apparent disasters of this world if that self is ever to transcend materiality.

Be not fainthearted because failure *seems* to be in thy way, or that self falters—but "how many times shall I forgive, or ask forgiveness—seven times?" "Yea, seventy *times* seven!" or, "not how I faltered, but did I seek His face again?"   281-7

For many may labor well under prosperous reactions and others well under adverse—but indeed greater is he who may take *all,* not merely as a part of the experience but using each for the abilities and opportunities for the greater manifestation of the sincerity of its purpose and its ideal.   1731-1

(Q) [993]: In passing through the test that has come with the sign that was promised, has my faith been sufficient? Would appreciate more light regarding same, and how I should act.

(A) As has been promised, "My grace is sufficient," and "Take no thought of what ye shall say in the hour of trial or test, for it will be given thee that as is necessary for the renewing of that spirit that makes for the understanding of 'His Spirit beareth witness with thy spirit.'" Then, meet each step as is shown thee, remembering that He has promised, "I am with thee always, even unto the end of the world. I will not leave thee comfortless, but will come to thee, and he that takes my cross shall not bear it alone." 262-15

(Q) How can I keep from worrying so much about my wife's health?
(A) Why worry, when ye may pray? Know that the power of thyself is very limited. The power of Creative Force is unlimited.
(Q) What qualities must I develop to grow more rapidly spiritually?
(Q) Patience! 2981-1

Remember, there has been given, "Fear rather him who may destroy body and soul than he who may destroy the body alone."
In an hour of trial, when there are influences abroad that would change or mar, or take away that freedom which is the gift of the Creative Forces to man; that man might by his own innate desire be at-one with God, the Father, as was manifested in Jesus, the Christ; there should be the willingness to pattern the life, the emergencies, the exigencies as may arise, much in the way and manner as the Master indicated to each and every soul.
According to the pattern of the life, as He gave, one should ever be able to give the evidence of the hope and faith that lies within the individual. 602-7

52 / Focusing

Attaining purposeful focus is basic to the achievement of cosmic unity. To attain this state one must develop control over the body and mind, so as to be able to see clearly the direction of the self to the immediate situation. But forget not the whole while focusing on the particular. To attend too carefully to the details might give one a distorted picture of what is really important.

Know first and foremost, as has been given, that the Lord thy God is *one!* Then know, too, that thyself is one—thy ego, thy I Am. Thy purposes, then; thy heart and thy life must be a *consistent* thing!

For if thine eye be single (the I Am; that is, the purposes, the desires—and ye work *at it!*), then thy *whole body* is full of light.   1537-1

And those influences in the emotions, unless they be governed by an ideal, often may become as a stumbling stone.

But use rather thy choices, thy endeavors, thy experiences, in a way and manner that they may become stepping-stones for a greater comprehension, a greater awakening of that consciousness of the Creative Forces of good, of hope, of faith, of brotherly love, of kindness, of gentleness; yea, of patience.   1599-1

(Q) Explain, "If thine eye be single, thy whole body shall be full of light." [Matt. 6:22, 23]

(A) It explains itself. The I AM, the I Self, the I Consciousness, the eye as in those things James has given; the eye that hath looked on, the eye that hath observed, the eye that hath desired in the heart. *That* eye.

If thine eye be single thine whole body is then full of light. Just as indicated in that given, as the Master gave to him that became the teacher to many peoples, how hard it is to kick against the pricks. Or in other words, how hard it is to make thine eye single, or thyself to say, "Lord, have *thy* way with me."   262-85

In the relations then with individuals, let those forces emanate that the self may ever be conscious of the life well spent in keeping the spiritual aspects of life first and foremost. Not that anyone should give self to being sober, long-faced or not knowing any of the pleasures of the earthly spirit, yet use, rather than abuse, those relations.   212-1

(Q) How can body avoid constant restlessness and sense of frustration and uselessness? Why doesn't her home life and her charities satisfy her?

(A) These will, when they are made one with the mental, physical and spiritual well-being; for these have been kept *separated*—and one as not knowing what the other did, but in the coordinating of the physical and mental and spiritual well-being, of that as may be accomplished in the home, in the charity, or in the associations socially, these should be *ever* with the eye single of that, "whatsoever my hands find to do, that will I do, with an eye single of showing, manifesting, living, *being*, my concept of the Divine."   454-1

53 / Growth

Conditons bode well, but there is the need for patience, for allowing things to progress as they should. This is no time to attempt to force issues. Progress is a gradual process. With firm commitment to one's place in the social order—even though it sometimes seems unexciting or unchallenging—this is still the direct and decisive approach to growth. Call upon your inner stamina to persevere in order to progress steadily.

(Q) Should I *learn* something, or have another work?
(A) This would be contrary to that just indicated. For these are all one. As life itself is one, so is the work one. The work in the present is a growing or a preparation for the next step. For ye are indeed (this is not merely philosophizing) gods in the growth. And as ye apply today, tomorrow's step is given thee.   1554-6

While storms and trials are necessary in every soul, as we see manifested in nature, only in contentment does *growth* make manifest. Not contentment to that point of satisfaction, for a satisfied mind or soul ceases to seek. But only in contentment may it receive and give out. In *giving* does a soul grow, even as a tree, even as a rock, even as a sunset, even as a world *grows* in its influence upon that about it. So has that force grown that we find manifested in the earth that we worship as constructive influence of God, as to the All-Wise purpose, or as to the Holy Spirit, or as to those influences that make alive in giving, in *making* itself manifest. So are ye gods in the making, saith He that walked among men as the greater teacher of all experiences and ages.   699-1

There is no standing still. Either one progresses or retards, and one that does not use *every* means for development and for gaining the better understanding of how to use that in hand is retarding. One that applies self in the manner of the pattern as is set in material only finds same magnified in the spiritual consciousness, see?

900-309

(Q) Has any progress been made in the last two or three incarnations?
(A) There is progress whether ye are going forward or backward! The thing is to move!   3027-2

And unless each soul entity (and this entity especially) makes the world better, that corner or place of the world a little better, a little bit more hopeful, a little bit more patient, showing a little more of brotherly love, a little more of kindness, a little more of long-suffering—by the very words and deeds of the entity, the life is a failure; especially so far as growth is concerned. Though you gain the whole world, how little ye must think of thyself if ye lose the purpose for which the soul entered this particular sojourn!   3420-1

(Q) Is the average fulfillment of the soul's expectation more or less than fifty percent?
(A) It's a continuous advancement, so it is more than fifty percent.   5749-14

Here one finds herself in a position where assertive behavior brings ruin, and where one lacks the position she feels deserving of. Forces beyond your immediate control have thrust you into a role or situation whose diverse elements do not really concern you personally. The sage, through her understanding and cosmic perspective, overcomes any self-pity. She keeps her internal focus on the ultimate goal of spiritual fullness and transcends any apparent unfairness in the situation.

For the law of the Lord is perfect, converting the soul, and the greater the stress, the greater the impress of the purposes upon the life of the Master, greater may be the joys which are found.

Do not let those things which may not in the present be understood weary thy soul, but know that sometime, somewhere, ye, too, will understand. Keep the faith.

5369-2

(Q) Considering my prejudice and feeling of unfairness concerning conscription, please advise me how to conduct myself so as to develop rather than retard through the experience?

(A) This has been indicated in the first premise. Consider Him—who is thy guide, thy way. Did He hold prejudice because of those in authority, or because there were those experiences that were displeasing among His own peoples, or among the followers and the officers of the house of the Lord?

He only filled that place—as ye may do. Use those ideals, those principles in thy daily activity.   1107-2

If there is still held that of self-pity, or the continued making for condemnation of self, such influences work as definitely upon the physical organisms as related to the sensory reactions as slow poison to the system.

1073-5

(Q) How can I overcome the feeling that I am most misunderstood?
(A) Be honest with self as you would have others be honest with thee. In that manner ye may overcome all those things that bring doubt or fear.   2509-2

. . . when there is that activity in which the apparent action of the self as in relationships to others is unappreciated for its phase of good or phase of material gain, there comes a hurt, there comes a disappointment . . .

And these become then periods in which the entity finds itself oft having to turn again to that which has been given; know in whom as well as in what ye have believed.   1554-2

There are barriers builded, yes. These may be taken away in Him, who has paid the price for thee; not of thyself but in faith, in love, in patience, in kindness, in gentleness may it be met.

That these have been the experience may appear to the entity as rather unfair. Is it? The law of the Lord is perfect. His grace is sufficient, if thy patience will be sufficient also.   5001-1

55 / Fullness

Conditions reach the optimum. Utilizing the cosmic fullness while it is within him, the sage sheds clear light on all within his reach. This is a time of abundance. But it is also wise to remember that the cycle must turn someday, and the mountain climber who does not cease to move must eventually start downward after reaching the summit. However, for today he can take with him the pride of achievement and the splendor of his vision from the mountaintop.

(Q) [69]: When one has gotten the understanding of the oneness with the Father-Mother-God, why is it one does not experience the joy and bliss, and overcome all inharmony, which is their divine birthright? May I have the answer from Master Jesus, if possible?

(A) Then, with patience wait for that. Is that attained in thine self so that the consciousness of the Master comes to thee in all thine hours, then with patience wait ye on the Lord; for as one finds that in the understanding of the oneness, when *He* has *found* that the vessel is worthy of acceptation it is *kept* full.   262-25

Then, know what thy ideal is; of the *spiritual* not of the temporal; not that around which there may be put metes and bounds, but rather put thy ideal in those things that bespeak of the continuity of life; the regeneration of the spiritual body, the revivifying of the temporal body for *spiritual* purposes, that the seed may go forth even as the Teacher gave, "Sin no more, but present thy body as a living sacrifice; holy, acceptable unto Him, for it is a reasonable service."

These things as an ideal should be founded in thine experience, as thou hast seen again and again the vision of the mountaintop yet these visions have faded because thou hast not founded thy ideal in the Creative Forces that are set in Him who gave, "As ye do it unto the least, ye do it unto me."   969-1

In the attitudes keep creative in thought, knowing that in Him is life and life more abundant to those who seek to do His bidding.

What is the first commandment with a promise? Said another way, it is life abundant. What is life? It is opportunity to serve the living God!   3524-1

To base the activities on the spiritual outlook does not mean that one should become sordid, self-centered or puritanic in any sense. Let each question be answered by determining what thy ideal should be respecting same.

The Christian principle is a joyous, abundant, happy, hopeful life in all phases of its experience, of its expression. And it only meets sorrow, disappointment and such with that assurance of peace and hope and life abundant.   270-48

. . . on the mountaintop, the entity gains the full height, or the full concept, of the manner and way in which the entity may and must act, would the entity gain the full understanding and the returns from same.

900-305

56 / Sojourning

In the odyssey of your life, you are always on your way to something. Like a traveler who is continually pursuing a better life, you constantly strive for what lies just beyond the glimpsed horizon. Your life mingles the joy of discovery with the restlessness of always searching for something. Often you seem to others as a stranger whose identity comes from a distant source.

Has God changed? Have ye wandered so far away? Know ye not that, as He has given, "If ye will be my children, I will be thy God"? and "Though ye wander far away, if ye will but call I will hear"? 281-41

When opportunities are presented, it is the entity's own *will* force that must be exercised—that which has separated it or has made it equal to the creative influences in the higher spiritual forces to make for itself that advancement. Then in *every* contact is there the opportunity for an entity, a soul, to fulfill or meet in itself or its soul self's association with the Creative Forces from the First Cause, to embrace that necessary for the entity to enter into the at-oneness with that Creative Force. Hence as for the entity's fulfilling, it is *ever* on the road.

903-23

. . . each cycle brings a soul-entity to another crossroad, or another urge from one or several of its activities in the material plane. But these are chosen with the purpose to indicate to the entity how and why those urges are a part of the entity's experience as a unit, or as a whole. For, one enters a material sojourn not by chance, but there is brought into being the continuity of pattern or purpose, and each soul is attracted to those influences that may be visioned from above. Thus *there* the turns in the river of life may be viewed.

To be sure, there are floods in the life; there are dark days and there are days of sunshine. But the soul-entity stayed in a purpose that is creative, even as this entity, may find the haven of peace as is declared in Him.

3128-1

The image of Him is within thine own self, if ye will but open thy heart, thy mind, thy conscience to the in-dwelling of that force, of that promise which is thine own—if ye will but embrace same.

In those abilities of thy mental and material self, then, pattern same after His manner of expressing same be-fore His fellow man. For ye are indeed the fellow traveler with Him.

1796-1

For each entity in the earth is what it is because of what it has been! And each moment is dependent upon another moment. So a sojourn in the earth, as indicated, is as a lesson in the school of life and experience. Just as it may be illustrated in that each entity, each soul-entity, is as a corpuscle in the body of God—if such an entity has applied itself in such a manner as to be a helpful force and not a rebellious force.

2823-3

57 / Penetrating Wind

A time for subtle penetration, like the wind that moves invisibly but with influence. Remain in the background as problems confront your life. By staying detached and not forcefully exerting your will, the quality of your character indirectly has a powerful effect.

One that fills the mind, the very being, with an expectancy of God will see His movement, His manifestation, in the wind, the sun, the earth, the flowers, the inhabitant *of* the earth.   341-31

We are conscious of the action of psychic and spiritual forces in the same manner we are conscious of the action of electrical forces in any manner in the physical world, or as we see, "The wind bloweth where it listeth. Thou heareth the sound thereof though know of from whence it cometh nor whence it goeth."   900-56

Let thy voice be raised, then, as in praise to thy Maker; not in word alone but rather in the manner in which ye meet thy fellow men day by day. For the prayer, and the living of same by those sixty and four who are here gathered, may even save America from being invaded—if that is what ye desire.   3976-25

Only in Him in whom there was found no guile, and though He were buffeted by man—though He was ridiculed by those in power, though He suffered among those convicted of crime in the flesh, and railings against their fellow man—yet those tenets as were proclaimed by that as the man, making self as the son of man, and through those conditions became the Son of the living God—in these tenets, in *these* ways and manners, may such conditions be brought to the realization of those that would *build* an invisible empire within the hearts of men ...   3976-4

(Q) Are there any entities in the invisible world who are trying or have tried to reach me with messages?
(A) Oft, as has been given, have there been *glimpses* of those innate forces and *influences* that would guide or direct, yet—as has been given—better that these be from those forces from within *self,* than from too *much* of those of the outside influence; for when the contacts may be made with the divine forces themselves, why take substitutes?   1048-1

(Q) Do I have any direct guidance from invisible helpers?
(A) As indicated, ever the guardian angel stands before the throne of God—for each individual.
Let not thy good be evil-spoken of nor thy bad be such as to cause continued questioning. Rather let the attitude be in that direction of hopefulness for the things to come.   3189-3

58 / Contentment

Contented pleasure is at every turn. But even in a time of joy, one must remain inwardly strong, aware of the direction of thoughts. It is so easy to relax, to let oneself flow contentedly with pleasure. If pleasure's route is away from the path, one may be swept along with it. Care must be taken to integrate this positive force so that it benefits both one's outward and inward growth.

Where, then, may this be accomplished? First that determination must be found in self's *own* mind, heart and soul; for, as the body knows, it is not *all* of death to die, neither is it all of life *just* to live! but to be of a service to someone else is the *only* way that life is made to be such as to bring contentment, and to find the joy, the pleasure in living.

Then, when such a determination has been reached, choose that surrounding (*wherever* it may be) which is most conducive to bring those conditions in the experience of the entity. *There* make the *physical* stand, that "Though the heavens may fall, though *my body may be racked with pain, I will conquer it here and now!*"

Only with such determinations may the body find that peace, that hope, that place where shadows do not fall, where joy and pleasure in well-being is the lot of the mental and material body. 911-7

In the study of ideal and idealism, as it may be termed, well that the ideal be outside one's self—rather than for the motives of same be as added, in any manner, to the pleasure, satisfaction, gratification, contentment, ease, or such. Rather in humbleness, drawing a comparison of self's own activities as related to the ideal as is set or held, then individualities and the application of the things of life may be gained or attained.   301-3

Then, in the mental-soul balance of the entity, there are abilities in many directions that in the application of same to self may make for influences that may bring into self contentment or joy, or may at times make for those very same influences in self where the pleasure may be in those of relationships to others rather than of looking too closely within self's own relation or activity.   491-1

Do these things; *live* these things, that contentment may come; not being satisfied, no—but grow in these things. For, as ye nourish and cherish these things in thy dealings with thy associates, thy fellow man, faint not because thou dost feel at times that thou art not appreciated for thine efforts among thy associates or friends; but rather let those things that would make doubts or misunderstandings give place to love. Then thou shalt find in thine experience in life that this world's goods, whether little or much, are replaced with that in self and with that which is said concerning thee—that cannot be bought with money, fame, position, or with powers that make men afraid.   531-3

59 / Flowing Dispersion

The wise person knows that often it is only through separating oneself from the apparent flow of worldly life that true understanding can come. There are obstacles which must be dissolved before progress can be made. The sage knows how to disperse illusion with purifying waters of understanding.

Then, purify thy mind if ye would meditate. How? Depending on what is thy concept of purification! Does it mean to thee a mixing up with a lot of other things, or a setting aside of self, a washing with water, a cleansing or purifying by fire or whatnot?

Whatever thy concept is, be *true* to thine inner self. *Live* that choice ye make—*do it!* not merely say it but *do it!*

Purify thy body. Shut thyself away from the cares of the world. Think on that as ye would do to have thy God meet thee face to face. "Ah," ye say "but many are not able to speak to God!" Many, you say, are fearful. Why? Have ye gone so far astray that ye cannot approach Him who is all merciful? He knows thy desires and thy needs, and can only supply according to the purposes that ye would perform within thine own self.

Then, purify thy body, physically. Sanctify thy body, as the laws were given of old, for tomorrow the Lord would speak with thee—as a father speaketh to his children.

281-41

Study to show thyself approved unto God, rightly divining the words of truth, keeping self unspotted from the world. Though the world hate thee, be not *of* the world. Though things, conditions, appearances, may grow as to be red, dark, black—if thine heart, thine soul is founded in Him, the *dawn* shall come! 792-1

. . . do not look or seek for the phenomenon of the experience without the purpose, the aim. *Use* same as a criterion, as what to do and what not to do. Not that it, the simple experience, has made or set *anything* permanent! For there is the constant change evidenced before us; until the soul has been washed clean through that the soul in its body, in its temple, has *experienced* by the manner in which it has acted, has spoken, has thought, has desired in its relationships to its fellow man!

518-2

. . . keep the self unspotted from the world; that is, do nothing physically or in thought—that you'll be ashamed to present to thy Maker or to the woman you love. Don't be ashamed, and don't ask others to do something that you would not do yourself nor to be something that you are not yourself. Then keep the self unspotted from the world. This should not be as your system or policy but it should be your religion. For all that you may know of God is within yourself. What are you doing about it? What are you doing with it? 3689-1

60 / Limitation

Restrictions are necessary in our world. The sage realizes the limits of her ability, lives within those limits, and thereby gains her freedom. But neither too great nor too small restrictions are satisfactory. To be able to determine what is proper, the sage defines a personal code of ethics, rooted in her ideals. Once she has articulated this means of measurement, she can define the boundaries of her behavior in a manner which guides but does not frustrate.

Know, as has been given, God looks on the heart, not on the outward appearance. A rose by any other name may be just as sweet. So may an individual by any name. What is the purpose? The church, the God-force, is within self; not in the name that may be added by man. That oft becomes the stumbling stone to man. For to such there is limitation, and who can limit God? Who would limit the Master? Who would limit self, in God's direction?   3350-1

There has also come a teacher who was bold enough to declare himself as the son of the living God. He set no rules of appetite. He set no rules of ethics, other than "As ye would that men should do to you, do ye even so to them," and to know "Inasmuch as ye do it unto the least of these, thy brethren, ye do it unto thy Maker." He declared that the kingdom of heaven is within each individual entity's consciousness, to be attained, to be aware of—through meditating upon the fact that God is the Father of every soul.   357-13

(Q) Although the upward flight of my soul has been

tremendous, why has it always been blocked by limitation when opportunity has come?

(A) . . . True, each soul as it enters this material plane enters for its advancement.

What the soul-entity does about that it has gained in experience, in application, makes for whether this is to be far—or very little—or even a backward tend. For growth is hindered as by the searing of influences that are not of the nature to make quick or lasting growth.

708-1

(Q) What are my present errors in conducting my personal life and my work?

(A) As has been indicated, a little more patient, a little more tolerant, a little more humble. But, as has been indicated, not a tolerance that becomes timid—this would make rebellion in self. Not a patience that is not positive.

Not an humbleness that becomes morbid or lacking in beauty. For as orderliness is a part of thy being, so let consistency—as persistency—be a part of thy being.

1402-1

Don't abuse that intuition, but know that in the use of same, it must follow the pattern of the law and there must be ideals as well as rules and regulations, and that in the application of the tenets innately in self from the intuitive forces they must be for the common good of all and do not use to take advantage of thy brother, or as for satisfactions.

5163-1

61 / Sincerity

When one must deal with difficult people, he should concentrate on being internally firm and externally gentle. In this way, he can manifest the penetrating understanding necessary for fruitful communication. Through sincere discussion, the sage gains knowledge needed to make a truly just response, thereby averting disharmony.

(Q) Please advise Gladys Davis if there are better methods of handling the work which comes under her supervision.

(A) Only don't find fault so often. Look within self. And ye can create, ye can add to, ye can *stimulate sincerity* in the minds and in the hearts of thy helpers—who will be entirely changed in less than sixty days and you have it all to do over again! So begin with self first. Be sincere. Be patient. Be gentle, be kind. And let each understand that to *someone* this means life and death, hope and despair, and that if this were thine only channel for help what should be thy attitude? 254-115

It is not what one knows that counts, but what one does about that it knows! Then it is the application of these attributes to which this soul, each soul, must adhere—to prevent confusion, to bring about harmony, to bring about not gratifying at all times but contentment in the experience; that first of sincerity of purpose, that of long-suffering with others, that of patience with self, that of understanding of others' viewpoints—and seeing thyself as others see thee in the light of that thou proclaimest to others that thou believest. 1182-1

Be kind, be gentle, be patient. For he that waiteth on

the Lord in patience, in sincerity, in honesty, shall not be lacking in principle nor in opportunity—either in the material things or in the peace that brings the more perfect understanding.   1983-1

Remember, fame and fortune and power are not the rule, but sincerity, patience, kindness, long-suffering, gentleness. Against these there is no law, for it *is* the law—of love, of knowledge, of wisdom.   189-3

But impress upon self, and upon *all,* that the body is associated or affiliated with not a goody-goody attitude but being purposefully good *for something!*
Parade not thy ideals. Be humble. Be gentle. Be kind. Be sincere.
Be true to self, to self's obligations, to self's promises; that there may be within *self* the purpose to meet all factors—good, bad, indifferent—in such a manner that the *experience* may be for betterment of *every* nature, for every member of the family—as well as those ye meet day by day.   934-6

Then, according to how thoroughly ye live up to them, is to how much peace, how much harmony, how much development ye will find in this experience. For sincerity and consistency are real virtues; and in a woman, sincerity is indeed a jewel, for in a man, it rarely exists!
                                          2175-8

62 / Humility

Engage only in activities in which you are competent. Enjoy success in modest endeavors. To overreach will meet with grief. In such times as these, the sage manifests simplicity and humility in her behavior. In this way, she is not diverted from her path.

(Q) Why do I blush so noticeably whenever I become suddenly or unexpectedly the focus of attention?

(A) Because of keeping self subdued in its positions of activity throughout. As indicated, put self to the front, yes—but in the *power* of the Divine. No one blushes when speaking with Him. 3343-1

Who, having named the name of the Christ, has become conscious of that He represented or presented in the world? As the records have been handed down that Abraham represents the faithful, Moses meekness, David the warrior yet humility, so the Christ represents love; that all may know that He hath paid the price for all. 262-56

(Q) Is our lack of material necessities due to the fact that we have not first sought the Kingdom, or lack of faith in not speaking the word?

(A) Both. For what saith the law? Seek ye first the Kingdom of God and all things shall be added unto thee thou hast *need of!* Most of us think we need a great deal more than we do!

When there was given the bounty to man through the activities of the law of the Lord, did He prepare other than that needed for the sustenance of all? In the preparation at the feast of Galilee in Cana what supplied He? The meats and the viands of the table? No, only that lacking. When He supplied the needs to the thousands that were weak and ahungered and troubled, did He use other than that at hand? That *at hand* was multiplied in the blessings!

Be patient, all. For all will pass through, in material experience, the greatest bounty of all. When ye fail here or there, ye must learn thy lessons. Humility, patience, faith. 262-89

Not with that outward show which may be experienced by attempting to solve some problem that there may be the enjoying of the reward for same, but rather that there may be the experiencing of the joy, the happiness, the harmony, the love, that fruit which comes from recognizing and using the privileges that are for those who—in their simplicity of manner recognize, know, experience His presence; which abides with thee, wilt thou but recognize, understand its own closeness to thee in thine daily experiences. In this manner, then:

In putting into practice that thou knowest to do, in the *little* things, being led by that which has been *given* to each, thy contributions may be such from this as to aid others who may seek to know His presence, the joy of His presence, the harmony, the peace that comes with abiding in Him. 262-33

63 / Completion

The river is crossed; the task is fulfilled. You feel the joy of completion and the end of tensions that beset you in the struggle to cross over. For this grand achievement, the forces in your life have come into harmony. But this moment of fulfillment is also the first moment of falling apart. It is a turning point when the energy begins to disperse. In the midst of your feeling of completion, be prepared to gather yourself and begin anew the never-ending effort.

(Q) Have I known [ex-husband] in previous lives, was the marriage a karmic debt and is it now finished?

(A) It is now finished. There was much to be worked out. It is complete in itself, but will be met again in another experience.   2185-1

It is not that which causes the uprising or the tumult or the shout, nor the voice of the trumpets for the mighty, that brings accomplishment within one's own self. These are not God's ways. Rather in the stillness of the night, in the still small voice, in the beauty in the smile of the babe, in the beauty of the blush of the rose, do we find those activities that play upon the hearts and sentiments of men and women everywhere! These are the things that wield the greater power among the masses as well as those that rule in power and in might.

And know, as ye learned in those experiences, there is no power given to any man—nor to thyself—save by the will of the Creative Force as an opportunity that he may become more aware of the glory and the purpose of God's ways with man!   1641-1

(Q) Please advise her spiritually and mentally for her complete happiness and accomplishment of life's work.

(A) Keep in the ways that are known to self, and that are satisfying to the desires of the spiritual life; the aid as may be given in counsel and advice to those about the body; worrying as little as possible as to the manner in which the responses are made to such; knowing in self that the seed of thought sown in the advice, whether there is built a resentment at the time or not, *will* if self does *not* build a wall of resentment—sooner or later have its effect upon those about it.   325-44

(Q) Must the solar cycle be finished on earth, or can it be completed on another planet, or does each planet have a cycle of its own which must be finished?

(A) If it is begun on the earth it must be finished on the earth. The solar system of which the earth is a part is only a portion of the whole. For, as indicated in the number of planets about the earth, they are of one and the same—and they are relative one to another. It is the cycle of the whole system that is finished, see?   5749-14

You are on the edge of an important change. The crossing of the river is still ahead of you—a challenge full of possibilities and dangers. In such times, the sage avoids the bravado of overconfidence. Instead, she waits and accumulates energy in order to be prepared for the efforts that lie ahead.

(Q) Any other advice at this time?

(A) Love the Lord, eschew evil. Do not find faults nor look for faults in either. Not that they do not exist, and that thou art not conscious of same; but more and more become conscious of the beauty in each. And we will find happiness, joy.

Sorrow, hardships—yes; but glory rather that these make for a *new day,* a new opportunity for each to be the stay as for the other in *their* seeking as one to be a channel of blessings to others.   688-4

(Q) Is there anything in particular I can do now to accomplish the reason for present incarnation?

(A) If there hadn't been you wouldn't be allowed to be in the earth in the present! These become self-evident facts in themselves, or should, to those who apply themselves: belief in God, belief in self, belief in the divinity of man's relationship to God, accomplished for, by and through one, Jesus the Christ. The belief, the faith, the doing of that thy hands find to do which is in accord with, in compliance with His desires, gives reason, gives purpose, accomplishes that. For what were His words? "Father, I come to thee, I have finished the work thou gavest me to do." Hast thou finished the work He gave thee to do; hast thou sought to know the work? Hast thou walked and talked with Him oft? It is thy privilege. Will ye?   3051-7

There are faults; there are virtues. Magnify in thy life and thy experience all the virtues, as love, hope, brotherly kindness, gentleness, patience. This ye need to guard closely as a teacher, as an instructor, and that ye need to use, particularly in that in which ye may do the best, in thy writing. While you may never set the world on fire, you may change the opinions of masses.   5214-1

Be sure there is not too much difference made in ideas and ideals, for, as has so oft been given, these must of necessity, for the accomplishment of the purport of teaching, training, and giving to a waiting world the individual truths as may be exemplified in the individuals' lives, until that or those individuals may become one with that purport as is being set forth—an *idea* may be beautiful, may be wonderful, but without the background of an *ideal* becomes as but sounding brass, or as the gourd without water.

In these things, then, let each be mindful of that place, that niche, that purport each is to fill, and *fill* that with *all* of the power, might, strength, that lies within that body!   254-50

Appendix 1 / Summary Chart of Hexagrams

upper \ lower	☰	☳	☵	☶	☷	☴	☲	☱
☰	1	34	5	26	11	9	14	43
☳	25	51	3	27	24	42	21	17
☵	6	40	29	4	7	59	64	47
☶	33	62	39	52	15	53	56	31
☷	12	16	8	23	2	20	35	45
☴	44	32	48	18	46	57	50	28
☲	13	55	63	22	36	37	30	49
☱	10	54	60	41	19	61	38	58

Appendix 2 / Scripts for Two Guided Experiences

Although synchronicity cannot be caused, created, or manipulated, we can still look for ways to sensitize ourselves to its occurrence. The following two scripts—which can certainly be changed and adapted to meet your own needs—can create an effective guided imagery experience.

Read over them both. Perhaps you'll find that one appeals to you more than the other. The first is less visual and more focused on specific suggestions to your unconscious mind. It also includes a prayer related to greater sensitivity to synchronistic guidance. It's designed to be used during the second week of the personal research project described in chapter 7.

The second script is a guided imagery experience which has a similar purpose but contains more visual suggestions. The second one is particularly geared to preparation to use the I Ching. It's designed for use during the third week of the personal research project.

You'll need to create an audiotape recording of the scripts. Read these words slowly into a tape recorder. Or, if you find the sound of your own voice distracting, ask a friend or family member to record this script for you. Each meditative experience should take ten minutes or more, so make sure the reading isn't hurried.

Although these two experiences are especially geared to the steps of the research project in chapter 7, they can be used informally whenever you sense the need to reattune yourself to the direction and guidance that comes from meaningful coincidences.

Script #1

First of all, choose a quiet place where you won't be disturbed for the next several minutes and just sit comfortably. Now, as you feel the quiet of the room around you, close your eyes and just breathe deeply and smoothly for a moment. You needn't force your breath into any rhythm, just let it find its own natural flow. With every cycle of inhalation and exhalation imagine that you become more and more relaxed. Allow your breath to put you in touch with the natural rhythms of life. It's as if the whole universe is breathing with you.

As you breathe in and out, you feel connected with the heaving of ocean waves and the gentle sigh of wind on a spring day. As you hear the flowing in and flowing out of your breath, you seem to hear also the gentle splashing of waves and the rustling of pine trees in the wind. Take a moment now and allow your breathing to merge more and more with this universal rhythm of life.

This gentle rhythm flowing through you has a very relaxing effect on you. You feel embraced and supported by this universal breath. It seems to flow through your whole body, relaxing every muscle and nerve. You notice particular parts of your body responding to this heave and sigh of the universe.

You feel a relaxation behind your eyes. This relaxation expands, releasing the muscles in the face and the head. Then you feel the muscles in your neck and shoulders loosening as all tension melts away. This relaxation continues down your back, loosening every vertebra. As this happens, your body feels more and more buoyant, as if you could actually float through the air. You're supported by this universal breath. You feel your knees relax, then your ankles, and finally your toes. Your whole body feels relaxed and alive and aware of the living breath of the universe, flowing in and around you.

You feel connected, you feel one with all creation. In this state, you become aware that all things in the universe are born of one Creator. This Creator is the spirit of love. All things are its children; therefore, all things are related to one another. Furthermore, you become aware that this Creator, this spirit of love, is mindful of all its children. Everything that happens in the universe is noted by the Creator. All things are noted within the mind of the Creator.

This is a very comforting realization. For you know that the Creator is also mindful of you. You are known and loved by this universal parent. What's more, there is a plan and purpose to your life. You are who and where you are not by chance but by design and purpose. Ultimately, your purpose is to manifest this spirit of love to all those you contact throughout the day. Only you can fulfill this purpose through your particular time and space. Your experiences and relationships are all a part of this plan and purpose. Nothing happens by accident. Everything that happens is somehow related to your unfolding purpose and destiny.

In this quiet time of reflection, you realize that the
oneness and purposefulness of life are true. You realize
that the events which happen to you are always meaningful. You realize that there is meaning and insight to
be gained in even those events that seem random or ac-
cidental. Therefore you offer a prayer to the Creator of
the universe and the Creator of you. You ask for help in
recognizing the meaningfulness of life's events. You offer
this prayer:

> Creator of the universe, be mindful of me and
> help me in my search for the meaning and purpose
> of life's experiences. Help me to recognize the com-
> mon thread of meaning to the seemingly random
> events of my day. And loving Creator, help me as I
> try to sift out the guidance that is available to me
> through these meaningful relationships. Guide my
> search. Help me through this study to fulfill my pur-
> pose and destiny in the earth. I know You are mind-
> ful of me. I know You love me. I have faith in Your
> power to guide and direct my life.

As you finish this prayer, you feel a new sense of vitality. You feel supported and directed by the living rhythm
of the universe. You feel keenly aware of the interconnectedness of all things. You feel a new consciousness of universal directness. You feel the abiding presence
of the creative spirit of love. Now your awareness begins
to return to your breathing. You become aware of the
gentle ebb and flow of breath filling and emptying your
lungs. You become conscious of your body located in this
space and time. You feel completely refreshed and alive.
When you're ready, you can open your eyes. You now feel
completely awake and alert, yet you also feel in tune with
the rhythm of the universe. Your consciousness is prepared to observe the meaningful relationships that bind

together the separate events of your day. You're also prepared to search out any possible message or guidance that may lie behind these synchronous events.

Script #2

This guided visualization experience is designed to prepare you for an optimum experience when you consult with the I Ching. In this reverie, I'm going to guide you on an imaginary journey. You'll begin the journey with a specific question in mind, and you will end as you pose that question to a holy master; a wise man or woman. The question you pose will be that one that you intend to ask using the I Ching. Therefore, if you don't have that question clearly in mind, pause the tape now and formulate the question. When you have it clearly worded, place your copy of the I Ching along with coins, note pad, and pencil near you, ready to be used at the close of the guided imagery experience.

Now sit comfortably in a quiet place where you won't be disturbed for the next several minutes. Close your eyes, and take a moment to settle into where you're sitting. Begin to feel the specialness of this time as it gathers around you and enfolds you. Put away any distracting thoughts. For the next few minutes you have no obligations, nothing is calling for your attention.

You're completely free to focus entirely on the sanctity of this moment. Your daily concerns are fading behind you. You feel yourself moving forward into new and uncharted experiences. You feel newly born, bright and fresh; like a butterfly emerging from its cocoon. With every breath you feel more and more liberated from the confines of your regular routine. With every breath you feel lifted out of the ordinary. You feel transported to a new place and a new time.

Slowly, a scene begins to emerge in your mind's eye.

You're standing alone at sunrise on the ocean shore. Over the ocean you can see the sun just breaking the horizon and splashing its orange light across the water. You hear the breaking waves. The air is cool but the rising sun feels warm on your face. You've come here for a moment of solitude and reflection.

There is a particular question in your mind that you've been struggling to resolve. You've weighed the various alternative answers to the question, yet you still feel uncertain and undecided concerning this situation in your life. You wish you had someone to talk to about this matter. Someone who would have profound insight and understanding... both of your feelings and of the situation.

And as you stand on the beach, musing on these thoughts and looking out over the ocean, you notice something in the distance. At first it seems like just a dot on the horizon, but as it comes nearer you see that it's a tall, masted sailing ship. It sails closer and closer to you. Soon you can see it clearly. It has three masts with square rigging. It's completely white with very graceful and beautiful lines. Soon it anchors just a few hundred yards from the shore. It looks majestic yet very friendly.

Then a small boat descends from the ship. The boat has three people in it, all dressed in white robes. Two of them begin rowing toward you and the third kneels at the bow of the boat waving to you and smiling. You then realize that the one waving to you is a woman with beautiful long hair and a friendly smile. Finally the boat brushes against the sand of the beach, and the young woman calls you by name and invites you into the boat. At first you hesitate; you ask her who she is and why she's inviting you into the boat. Her only reply is this, "You have asked in your heart to meet with a counselor who can help you resolve your mission. If you desire, I will take you to this person."

The gentleness in her voice and the sincerity in her

face convince you to accept her invitation. You find your-self being hoisted into the white, three-masted sailing ship. The deck of the ship is spotlessly clean and white. The sailors are both men and women who perform their duties effortlessly. You're surprised to notice that there is complete silence on board. All you hear is the wind in the sails and the splashing of the sea. Your guide leads you to a bench at the bow of the boat and instructs you to wait there until the journey's end.

As you sit there with the eastern sun warming your face, you begin to feel excited and exhilarated in antici-pation of meeting this wise counselor. You feel the gentle rocking of the ship as it glides across the calm water. The ocean spray cools your face. Eventually, you see land breaking the horizon as it comes nearer. You can see that it is a small green island with a single mountain rising up from its center. The ship continues to sail directly toward this island, and soon you hear the splashing of an an-chor as the ship perches just a few hundred yards from the shore.

Your guide stands beside you and invites you once again into the small boat which will carry you to the is-land. As the boat rows toward shore, you ask your guide, "Is this where I will meet the wise counselor?" Looking into your eyes, she says with a warm smile, "It is." As the boat scrapes the beach sand, you both climb out. You ex-pect to see the counselor waiting for you on the beach, but that person is not there. You turn to your guide and ask, "Where is the counselor?"

She turns to the center of the island, lifts her eyes, and says, "There. In order to meet this person, you must first climb the mountain of commitment." You hadn't ex-pected this obstacle. Yet, after such a long journey, you're quite ready to go this extra mile in order to receive the counselor's advice.

Your guide shows you a path and promises to wait for

you on the beach until you return. She gives you a fond
embrace and wishes you well. You turn to the path and
begin to climb. At times the way is steep and your legs
grow weary. However, after a short rest you begin again
your climb up the mountain.

Finally your path leads you to a small clearing which
stands before an opening in the side of the mountain.
Standing in this clearing is a white-haired individual
with a kindly face, who calls you by name and invites you
to sit together under a nearby tree. As you both settle into
the grass, you are offered some fruit. As you eat together
under the tree, you begin talking to the counselor about
the concerns of your life. You particularly discuss the issues that have been on your mind as the sun rose over
the ocean. The wise counselor at first just listens and
nods in understanding, looking at the ground. Finally,
you pose that carefully worded question which you have
come all this way to ask. Pose that question to the counselor now. As you wait to hear the words of advice, the
counselor turns and faces you. You look into the eyes of
this sage and you sense in them a deep wisdom. As you
search the depth of these eyes, you hear the counselor's
words, saying: "Help which will lead you to your own
answer is coming soon; be alert for it." You feel a comfort
in these words, and as the counselor smiles at you, the
scene begins to fade.

You slowly and gently begin to float back to this time
and place. Yet you feel the presence of this wise counselor abiding with you, even as you return to your awareness of here and now. You feel again your breathing
which is low and relaxed. You feel refreshed and ener-
gized, yet you're still eager to hear the advice of the wise
counselor. When you're ready, open your eyes and consult the I Ching, posing to it that same question which
you asked the counselor.

Bibliography

Aziz, Robert. *C.G. Jung's Psychology of Religion and Synchronicity.* Albany, N.Y.: S.U.N.Y. Press, 1990.

Huang, Kerson and Rosemary. *I Ching.* New York, N.Y.: Workman Publishing, 1987.

Lee, Jung Young. *Embracing Change: Postmodern Interpretations of the I Ching from a Christian Perspective.* Cranbury, N.J.: Associated University Presses, 1994.

Progoff, Ira. *Jung, Synchronicity, and Human Destiny.* New York, N.Y.: Julian Press, 1973.

Reifler, Sam. *I Ching.* New York, N.Y.: Bantam, 1974.

Ritsema, Rudolf, and Karcher, Stephen. *I Ching.* Rockport, Mass.: Element Books, 1994.

Shelburne, Walter. *Mythos and Logos in the Thought of Carl Jung.* Albany, N.Y.: S.U.N.Y. Press, 1988.

Wilhelm, Richard, and Baynes, Cary. *I Ching.* Princeton, N.J.: Princeton University Press, 1967.

Books of Related Interest:

Discovering Your Soul's Purpose by Mark Thurston.
ISBN 0-87604-157-8 paperback Order #324 $12.95

Dreams—Your Magic Mirror by Elsie Sechrist.
ISBN 0-87604-107-1 paperback Order #470 $15.95

How to Interpret Your Dreams by Mark Thurston.
ISBN 0-87604-107-1 paperback Order #292 $11.95

The Inner Power of Silence: A Universal Way of Meditation by Mark Thurston.
ISBN 0-87604-364-3 paperback Order #482 $12.95

Paradox of Power: Balancing Personal and Higher Will by Mark Thurston.
ISBN 0-87604-208-6 paperback Order #335 $10.95

Understand and Develop Your ESP by Mark Thurston.
ISBN 0-87604-097-0 paperback Order #287 $6.95

Your Mind: Unlocking Your Hidden Powers by Henry Reed.
ISBN 0-87604-365-1 paperback Order #480 $14.95

To order any of these books or to receive a free catalog, call us at

1-800-723-1112
Or write

A.R.E. Press
Sixty-Eighth & Atlantic Avenue
P.O. Box 656
Virginia Beach, VA 23451-0656

DISCOVER HOW THE EDGAR CAYCE MATERIAL CAN HELP YOU!

The Association for Research and Enlightenment, Inc. (A.R.E.®) was founded in 1931 by Edgar Cayce. Its international headquarters are in Virginia Beach, Virginia, where thousands of visitors come year round. Many more are helped and inspired by A.R.E.'s local activities in their own hometowns or by contact via mail (and now the Internet!) with A.R.E. headquarters.

People from all walks of life, all around the world, have discovered meaningful and life-transforming insights in the A.R.E. programs and materials, which focus on such areas as holistic health, dreams, family life, finding your best vocation, reincarnation, ESP, meditation, personal spirituality, and soul growth in small-group settings. Call us today on our toll-free number:

1-800-333-4499

or

Explore our electronic visitor's center on the
INTERNET: http://www.are-cayce.com

We'll be happy to tell you more about how the work of the A.R.E. can help you!

> A.R.E.
> 67th Street and Atlantic Avenue
> P.O. Box 595
> Virginia Beach, VA 23451-0595